THE Language BOOK

Andrew Mayne · John Shuttleworth

Hodder & Stoughton
A MEMBER OF THE HODDER HEADLINE GROUP

Cataloguing in Publication Data is available from the British Library.

ISBN 0 340 654651

First published 1996
Impression number 10 9 8 7 6 5 4 3 2 1
Year   1999 1998   1997 1996

Typeset and design by Mind's Eye Design, Lewes.

Printed in Great Britain for Hodder & Stoughton Educational, a division of Hodder Headline Plc, 338 Euston Road, London NW1 3BH by Redwood Books, Trowbridge, Wiltshire.

CONTENTS

PREFACE

Our aim in this book has been to make a wide range of Language Studies accessible to students moving from Key Stage 3 to Key Stage 4. The material covers comprehensively the area of 'Knowledge about Language' which remains an important element of the National Curriculum in English. Above all, this is a book that we hope will lead to lively and successful learning in the classroom.

The order of the chapters in *The Language Book* forms a coherent course of study, but each chapter has been designed to be 'free-standing', so that teachers may, if they wish, introduce topics in any sequence of their own choice.

The activities we have created for students to follow in *The Language Book*, deriving from both whole-class sessions and work in smaller groups, offer wide scope for the generation of written coursework for GCSE English and for the varied kinds of discussion that will provide good opportunities for oral assessment.

Andrew Mayne and John Shuttleworth

WORD GAMES

Most people enjoy playing games with words. There's hardly a newspaper that doesn't have its own crossword, and these can range from the fiendishly difficult to ones that can be polished off in a five-minute break. We've probably all played Scrabble at some time or other; indeed, it's reputed to be the Queen's favourite game. And there are lots of other word games that are sold commercially: two of the best known at the moment are Pictionary and Dingbats. So word games are popular!

We've given you the chance to play (and invent) some word games throughout this book. So whenever you see the juggler, take a break, puzzle over the brain teasers and perhaps even invent a few to baffle family and friends. You might even hit upon one that makes your fortune!

Chapter One

CHANGES IN MEANING

Words can be slippery customers! Meanings never seem to stand still and can therefore leave us very puzzled at times. What we're looking at in this section is how the meaning of words can change over time. There are three main reasons for these changes:

1 people stop using certain words;
2 existing words alter their meaning;
3 new words join the language.

Let's look at some examples of these three processes.

1 PEOPLE STOP USING CERTAIN WORDS

Here are fifteen words from each of four topic areas. Some of these words are no longer used in everyday life. You have to decide which these are.

CLOTHES	TRANSPORT	ENTERTAINMENT	FOOD
crinoline	tram	bingo	chitterlings
spats	hansom	cabaret	hamburger
wimple	estate car	gramophone	victuals
jodhpurs	pantechnicon	cribbage	pemmican
jeans	caravan	playhouse	pottage
plus-fours	convertible	ping-pong	blancmange
frock	brougham	juke box	risotto
bloomers	velocipede	disco	tuck
stetson	omnibus	revue	mutton
tank-top	taxi	phonograph	gruel
shawl	dormobile	video	galantine
stomacher	jeep	walkman	kedgeree
basque	bassinet	wireless	fool
waistcoat	roadster	nickelodeon	spaghetti
pullover	tricycle	cinema	junket

Each member of the group should work on one of the lists of words. Then:

1   Look up in a dictionary the meaning of any word you don't know and note it down.

2   Try to decide for each of the words in your list if it:

   a) is no longer used nowadays (hint: if the dictionary entry has (*obs.*) or (*arch.*) meaning *obsolete* or *archaic*, then the word is unlikely to be in use). Your dictionary might also tell you when the word was first used;

   b) might occasionally be used;

   c) is in general use today.

3   When you have put each word into one of the categories, discuss your findings with the other members of your group. Did you have any problems deciding whether a word had dropped out of use, or whether new words have joined the language to replace ones that are not used any more?

2 EXISTING WORDS ALTER THEIR MEANING

A public *convenience*?

Words never stay still! They are forever changing in meaning – sometimes very subtly so that we don't always notice it happening, sometimes quite abruptly. Take a word like *convenience* as an example of subtle change. Originally it meant 'suitability', but in the nineteenth century it came to have the meaning 'toilet', and people began using *public conveniences*. In the 1960s, another meaning was attached to the word – 'easy to use' – so we now eat *convenience foods* or buy *convenience products*.

A more abrupt change can be seen in a word like *gay* which almost overnight became an accepted word for 'homosexual'; and what used to be its main meaning of 'happy' and 'jolly' faded into the background.

Sometimes words keep both the original and the new meanings, as in the two examples of *convenience* and *gay*. Sometimes, as you have already seen, words just drop out of use.

Here's a list of ten words that have altered in meaning over the years. We want you to research how their meanings have changed and to record your findings. We've done the first one for you.

WORD	EARLY MEANING	MODERN MEANING
bead	prayer	a ball forming part of a necklace
fond		
companion		
girl		
posy		
tide		
journey		
starve		
presently		
doctor		
cockpit		

Add to this list yourself. To do this, all you need to do is to browse through a good dictionary and look for words that have more than one definition. Then, see if any of these definitions are marked (*obs.*) for *obsolete* or (*arch.*) for *archaic*. This will give you a *clue* as to whether these words have changed their meaning. Incidentally, 'clue' itself could be one of the words you might look up. See if the words you look up have newer meanings as well.

Once you've got your list of words (or you could just use ours), there are lots of puzzles or games you could design to test other people's knowledge of their language. Here is just one suggestion.

Design a set of cards, each card containing your chosen word plus three definitions of it on one side. Two of the definitions should be ones you have made up, but which could possibly be right, and the third should be the true original or earlier meaning of the word. You could then use your set of cards in quizzes or Trivial Pursuit type games. Here's an example of one of these cards:

> **BEAD**
>
> 1 A medieval drink made out of milk and honey.
>
> 2 A type of prayer.
>
> 3 Imprisonment in the stocks (pronounced *be-ad*)

3 NEW WORDS JOIN THE LANGUAGE

New words are always entering the language. There are lots of reasons for this. For instance, inventions and new processes need new words, so there are lots of words about air travel that our great-grandparents would never have come across: *runway, flight controller* and *helicopter*, for example. What would they have made of computers and computer language?!

One problem with very new words is that we can't tell if they will stay in the language or just simply fade away. Words are forever entering the language and at an increasingly rapid pace. This next list of words is as up-to-date as is possible at the time we are writing this, but there is every chance that by the time you read this, the words may either be very common and everyone will know what they mean, or have failed to catch on and therefore nobody will know what they mean.

> All these words were used in late 1994. Your task, in pairs, is to decide what they mean and to write possible dictionary definitions for them. You may, of course, already know!
>
> 1 brollability
> 2 screenager
> 3 masculist
> 4 rockumentary
> 5 infotainment
> 6 ecotourism
> 7 telecroft
> 8 upskill
> 9 bonkbuster
> 10 desktopping

SHAKESPEARE – WILL'S WORD POWER

You will probably all have read or seen a Shakespeare play and may well have been puzzled by some of the words he uses. For example, here's a very short passage from *Romeo and Juliet*. A servant is clearing a room and says:

> *Away with the join-stools, remove the court cupboard, look to the plate. Good thou, save me a piece of marchpane, and as thou loves me, let the porter let in Susan Grindstone and Nell.*

There are some words here that you will no doubt not have come across before because people have stopped using them: *join-stools* (stools made by a joiner), *court cupboard* (a sideboard) and *marchpane* (marzipan) are unlikely to be in your vocabulary. There will also be other words and expressions that you will understand, but which you won't use in your conversation or writing: *Good thou*, *look to* and *away with*, for instance. Shakespeare wrote *Romeo and Juliet* in 1595, so it's not very surprising that there are some 'antique' words used.

Let's look at some more short examples from Shakespeare's plays to see the processes of meaning change at work. Read them through carefully.

1 What dost thou with thy best apparel on? (*Julius Caesar*)

2 By the lord, thou sayest true, lad, and is not my hostess of the tavern a most sweet wench? (*Henry IV, part 1*)

3 Tut, our horses they shall not see, I'll tie them in the wood; our vizards we will change after we leave them; and sirrah, I have cases of buckram for the nonce, to immask our noted outward garments. (*Henry IV, part 1*)

4 I pray you, sir, what saucy merchant was this that was so full of his ropery? (*Romeo and Juliet*)

5 Scurvy knave! I am none of his flirt-gills; I am none of his skainsmates. And thou must stand by too, and suffer every knave to use me at his pleasure. (*Romeo and Juliet*)

With your partner, we want you to decide which words you think have changed in their use. Again, you'll need a dictionary to help you with your research. You'll probably find that:

a) there are some words which are not used any more;

b) there are some words that are used nowadays, but very rarely;

c) there are some words that are used nowadays, but have changed their meaning from Shakespeare's time.

We've drawn up a chart for you to complete and have begun to fill it in, but watch out – you might find yourself arguing with your partner over which column you should put the words in. For instance, is *thou* not used any more? Or is it still used in prayer?

No Longer Used	Rarely Used	Meaning Change
dost	thou	suffer
	thy	
	apparel	

Don't think that this process of words changing their meaning or falling out of use is confined to the dim and distant past – it's happening all the time, even as you read this! We've already mentioned how *gay* has changed its meaning quite recently. But look at this next list of words. They are all informal terms of approval. But how many of them would you use today?

ace	super
bazzin'	wicked
jolly good	smashing
bad	great
first-rate	red-hot
fantabulous	wizard

By the time you read this, new terms of approval will probably have come into use. Which one do you use at the moment?

WHY DO WORDS CHANGE MEANING?

We've looked in general at the reasons words change their meanings. Now it's time to look at these processes in a little more detail. In the chart below, we've suggested nine causes of meaning change and given an example of each. Read them through carefully.

REASON	EXAMPLE
1 The thing that the word refers to changes.	*Ship* used to refer mainly to Viking longboats, but now refers to liners, trawlers and other types of sea-going vessels.
2 The thing that the word refers to stops being used.	We no longer use armour, so *morion*, a kind of helmet, is no longer used.
3 Inventions are developed and refined, and new words come into the language to name them.	We used to listen to the *wireless*, then to the *tranny*; today we listen to a *walkman*. What will it be tomorrow?
4 Sometimes we want to be polite when we talk about certain subjects.	Nowadays, we go to the *toilet*, *loo* or the *bathroom*; in earlier times, we might have gone to the *privy*, *water closet* or to the *offices*.
5 Redundancy: sometimes we have lots of words for the same thing. Some of them don't get used very often.	*Domicile* is used very rarely; normally, we would use *house* or *home*.
6 Words reflect changes in the way we live.	*Purchase* used to involve getting something by force; now it means getting something by paying money.
7 Words sometimes 'improve' their meaning. This process is known as **amelioration**.	*Nice* originally meant *foolish* or *stupid*; now it can mean *agreeable* or *pleasant*.
8 Words sometimes 'deteriorate' in meaning.	*Silly* originally meant *holy* or *innocent*. Now it means *stupid* or *foolish*.
9 Words can add a non-literal or metaphorical meaning to their original, literal one.	*Head* originally meant only a part of the body; now we can talk about the head of a school or of an organisation.

You've seen that words can undergo very great changes of meaning over time. For example, did you know that what you presumably do a lot of your writing with, a *pen*, originally meant a large feather? It can be very interesting to trace the stages that have led to the present-day meaning of a word from what, at first sight, might appear to be rather obscure origins. For example:

1   *pen* = a large feather ➡

2   feathers were once used to make writing instruments that used ink ➡

3   the word for feather (*pen*) was used for the writing instrument itself ➡

4   *pen* came to be used for a type of writing instrument that uses ink.

The original connection is thus hidden in the mists of time.

Here's a two part piece of research:

1

In the first column there is a list of words that have changed their meanings quite drastically. In the second column, you'll find a list of their original meanings, but the word and its meaning are not opposite each other. Your task is to match the word in the first column with its original meaning from column two. You'll notice that *pen* and *feather* are in the lists to give you a start.

miniature	go
wade	foolish
chassis	scatter seed
broadcast	knowledgeable
pen	parts of ruined buildings
bank	pleasure
frock	weight
cunning	household management
smug	feather
clue	neat
rubbish	window frame
lust	monk's garment
poise	ball of wool
economy	bench
fond	red-coloured

2

Your second task is to see if you can explain the reasons behind the changes in meaning just as we did in the *pen-feather* example. Try not to rely on inspired guesswork, but use a good dictionary in your research. Present your findings to the class as a wall-chart or a short talk.

BROADENING AND NARROWING

There are two important processes that can occur when words change their meaning over time. These processes work in opposite ways: sometimes the meaning of a word grows and expands; sometimes the meaning of a word shrinks and contracts. Students of language call the first process *broadening* and the second *narrowing*.

Let's look at these processes in action: in this next sentence, you'll be able to see words broadening in meaning.

I went to the *butcher's* yesterday, but had to leave my *dog* outside the shop.

If you look up *butcher* in a dictionary, you will find that it originally meant *killer of goats*. Of course, butchers nowadays sell all kinds of meat, not just one type, as in the original meaning. And few butchers today kill animals; they leave that to staff of the abattoir. *Dog* also illustrates this process of broadening of meaning: originally it meant one particular breed; today, the word refers to all breeds – dachshunds, labradors, collies, etc.

However, in this next sentence, the words in italics have narrowed in their meaning.

The *doctor* told me I was suffering from *influenza*, but he didn't think my *family* needed to send for the *undertaker* just yet.

Doctor once meant *teacher* or *learned man*, but has now narrowed to mean a learned man in medical matters. *Undertaker* meant at one time someone who managed any task, but has narrowed to mean someone who manages funerals. Look up *family* and *influenza* to see how they have narrowed.

This piece of research will give you the opportunity to explore the process of broadening and narrowing further. Each of the words in the following list has undergone one of these processes. By researching the origins of the word in a good etymological dictionary, decide whether the word has either broadened or narrowed. There are twenty-two words in the list: nine have narrowed (become more specialized in meaning); thirteen have broadened (become more general in meaning). Which are they?

cockpit	adder
girl	quarantine
deer	meat
holiday	accident
manufacture	fowl
guys	paper
navvy	junk
hoover	ledger
poison	science
pigeon	deodorant
charming	shambles

DON'T BE OFFENSIVE!

It is with great regret that I have to tell you that last night Mr Smith
> *died.*
> *passed away.*
> *breathed his last.*
> *expired.*
> *was taken.*
> *laid down his life.*
> *gave up the ghost.*

There are some things that we don't like talking about very much. Death is one of them. Many people find it upsetting to be too direct about such a subject and try very hard to avoid mentioning it or, if they have to, don't like to use the straightforward term *died*. Hence we have expressions like *passed away*. Words and expressions that are used to take the place of ones that are too direct, too negative or too offensive are known as **euphemisms**.

Euphemisms are another major source of changes of meaning in the language. Of course, we can always cope with what we find difficult or

unpleasant by making a joke of it. So Mr Smith might not *die*, but *pop his clogs, kick the bucket, go west, snuff it* or *croak*.

Euphemisms, then, cover up what we might call the unpleasant facts of life. Many Victorians thought that it was rather naughty and unpleasant to mention that a lady had *legs*. So they came to be referred to as *limbs*. Even pianos had their legs covered up and were referred to as limbs! We've already seen some of the euphemisms that are used for the toilet and we're sure you could add lots of humorous ones of your own!

Which euphemisms might be used for the highlighted words in the following sentences?

1   The soldiers **killed** thirty of the enemy yesterday.

2   Andrew had had too much to drink and wanted desperately to **urinate**.

3   Having just turned sixty, Sheila was considered to be **old**.

4   Helen was **sacked** two weeks ago.

5   Michael has been **having sex** with Judy for three months.

6   Ann had so many glasses of white wine that she was feeling **drunk**.

Let's look at euphemisms from the other side! They are still being invented to cover up unpleasant facts and thus subtly helping to change the meaning of words. Each one of these euphemisms was used very recently in British newspapers. What do you think they mean?

physically challenged   preventive detention

ethnic cleansing   friendly fire

hearing impaired   personnel downsizing

SUPERGHOSTS

If you saw the letters ZZL on their own, you'd be puzzled. But, of course, they're part of the word *puzzled*. NSW looks odd, until you come up with the *answer*. What words do the following sets of letters come from? Clue: all the words are to do with language.

NGU NGL DJE RITI CCE NTEN LLI ICIT CTUA CKNA

Variations

1   Make up some of your own 'superghosts' to tease friends. It'll be easier for them if you tell them what subject your words are connected with. Here are some suggestions: *football teams, music, animals, food.*

2   The first player names a letter. The second player adds a letter to it, either in front or behind. The first player adds another letter to the first two. The aim is not to complete a word. However, if a player is challenged and cannot think of a word containing the letters already chosen, he or she loses.

Chapter Two

CHANGES IN SPELLING

The thought of spelling probably raises all sorts of familiar pictures in your mind! You've all no doubt had pieces of written work back from your teacher with lots of **sp** in the margin, telling you that you'd made a spelling mistake. Or do any of these sound familiar? *'Write out the word correctly ten times!' 'Right! Now for a short spelling test!' 'Can't anybody spell properly in this class?'*

Obviously spelling can cause some pupils (and adults) problems. But why? One of the main reasons is to do with the changes that have taken place in the language in the past. We're going to be exploring some of the effects of these changes in this section.

BREAKING THE RULES!

Many people think that English words have always been spelt in the same way as they are today. But that's not true, as we'll see later. In the past, English spelling was constantly changing and it's only within the last 200 years that it's become relatively fixed.

Even today, however, certain writers are allowed to break the rules and not have **sp** on their work. Look at these examples from advertisements where spelling rules and conventions are being 'bent'.

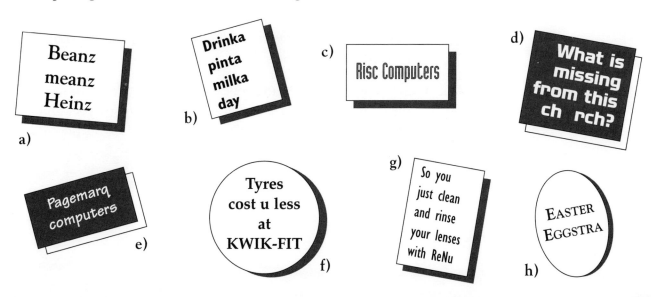

a) Beanz meanz Heinz

b) Drinka pinta milka day

c) Risc Computers

d) What is missing from this ch rch?

e) Pagemarq computers

f) Tyres cost u less at KWIK-FIT

g) So you just clean and rinse your lenses with ReNu

h) EASTER EGGSTRA

In your group, add to this collection of deliberate spelling 'mistakes'. There are many possible sources where you could find them in addition to adverts: notices, names of bands and singers, graffiti, fanzines and teenage magazines, for example. Why do you think 'mistakes' have been used in these types of writing? Do they have anything in common?

When you've collected some more (or you could use the ones we've given you), there are a number of linked investigations to make.

1 Decide which word(s) you would signal as **sp** if you were marking the work and what your 'correct' version would be.

2 Discuss and try to explain what spelling rules and conventions the writers have broken. To do this, you need to find other examples or words that follow the spelling pattern you are investigating, to prove that it *is* a pattern. For instance, you might say that *risc* ought to be spelt R-I-S-K because words that end with the K sound are spelt with a *k* at the end. For example: mask, task, quick, desk, tick, lick.

3 Explore further and see if you can find words that ought to follow your 'pattern', but don't, because they follow a different one which still, however, represents the same sound. For instance, if all K sounds were represented by a *k* at the end of the word, then we'd have *disk* instead of *disc*; *musik* instead of *music*; *mosk* instead of *mosque*. Can you think of any others?

4 Once your group has completed its investigations, report back on your findings to the whole class. You could, for instance, present them as a wall chart for display in primary school classrooms on *The Oddities of English Spelling*. Or you could prepare a short script to be broadcast on radio.

5 Try your hand at writing your own advertising slogans that break the normal rules of spelling. See how many your group can come up with. How about this for starters: Ruff-rider Jeanz for tuff guyz 'n' galz?

ALL CHANGE!

We've seen how advertisers break the rules when they want to. You might be surprised to learn, though, that there are people who want to push changes in spelling far beyond what the advertisers have done. These are the spelling reformers, and they have suggested some new systems. So you can see that even now, English spelling might be changed, if the reformers ever get their way. Reformers are nothing new, because even in 1568, Sir Thomas Smith wanted to expand the alphabet. With all this possibility of change in the air, who knows what this book would look like if it were published in 2100!

Let's have a look at some of the different ways that the reformers have tried to alter English spelling. Here are two short passages from different attempts at reforming our spelling. The first is about spelling, and the second is the opening of Abraham Lincoln's famous speech, the Gettysburg Address. Read them through carefully and then in groups, investigate the topics that follow.

1 New Spelling

At dhe furst glaans a pasej in eny reformd speling looks 'kwear' or 'ugly'. Dhis objekshon iz aulwaez dhe furst to be maed; it iz purfektly natueral; it iz dhe hardest to remuuv. Indeed, its efekt iz not weekend until dhe nue speling iz noe longger nue, until it haz been seen ofen enuf to be familyar.

2 World English Spelling

Forskor and seven yeerz agoe our faathers braut forthh on this kontinent a nue naeshon, konseevd in liberti, and dedikaeted to the propozishon that aul men ar kreeaeted eakwal.

Abraham Lincoln

> 1 Rewrite the passages in current English spelling. To make it easier for your group to compare the reformed version with the current one, you might want to write them out like this:
>
> At dhe furst glaans a pasej in eny reformd . . .
>
> = At the first glance a passage in any reformed . . .

2 Can you see why the reformers have changed particular spellings? Are there any patterns you can spot? It'll be helpful in this investigation not to think in terms of letters, but in terms of sounds. For instance, the letter **s** can have more than one pronunciation. Think of the sound of **s** in *is* or in *looks*. Or the sound of **a** in *any* or in *glance*. This might give you a clue about some of the changes.

3 Try writing in these new spelling systems. Here's some more from the passage used in *New Spelling*, but this time in Standard English. See if your group can rewrite it in *New Spelling*.

We instinctively shrink from any change in what is familiar; and what can be more familiar than the form of words that we have seen and written more times than we can possibly estimate?

What might be the objections to adopting a reformed system of spelling?

SILENT LETTERS

The main reason why people have been interested in changing the English spelling system is that, as you've no doubt already discovered, there are many oddities in it. In this next research topic, we'll investigate one of these oddities.

1

Some of the words in the following sentence contain 'silent' letters (letters which are not pronounced, but which are present nevertheless when the word is written). Can you spot these letters?

I doubt whether you know why the word cough is spelt C-O-U-G-H but is pronounced kof.

In fact, it would be much more logical to spell *cough* as *kof*. Just as *would* should (*shud*?) be *wud*. The whole sentence would probably be more sensibly written as:

I dout wether you no wy the word cough is spelt C-O-U-G-H but is pronounced kof.

Have a look at the next sentence and try to identify the silent letters in it.

On this island, in the fourteenth century, honest knights took great delight in building castles.

2

Let's see how many words we can find in English that contain silent letters. Working with a partner, try to list as many words as you can. To make it easier, we suggest you list your words under three headings:

a) words whose first letter is silent;

b) words whose central letter(s) are silent;

c) words whose final letter is silent.

To give you a start, we have begun to fill in a table for you.

First Letters	Central Letters	Final Letters
knight	is**l**and	lov**e**
wrong	rei**g**n	num**b**
psalm	hand**k**erchief	ke**y**
honest	p**s**alm	dam**n**

3

By now, you have probably listed many words with silent letters. But did you know that, of the twenty-six letters in the alphabet, only five are never silent? Try to work out which five they are. Remember they are all consonants.

A BRIEF HISTORY OF ENGLISH SPELLING

We've already suggested that some of the reasons for the oddities of English spelling stem from the past. It's now time for us to explore that past.

You know that there are twenty-six letters in the alphabet.

Did you know that there are forty-four separate sounds in spoken English?

PROBLEM

Not enough letters for all sounds!

SOLUTION

Some letters have to represent more than one sound, and some combinations of letters, like **th**, have to represent more than one sound.

Old English Spelling

Old English (or Anglo-Saxon) had twenty-seven letters in its alphabet and forty sounds in its pronunciation system. In the next exercise there are some Old English (OE) words whose pronunciation has changed only a little since that time. See if you can match them up with their modern English equivalents. For example, *cwen* is the OE word for *queen* and *sceap* is the OE for *sheep*.

OLD ENGLISH (OE)	MODERN ENGLISH
cwic	young
cirice	quell
cese	why
niht	church

brycg	what
hwy	night
sceap	tail
cwen	sheep
cwell	queen
cild	chin
milc	cheese
cinn	child
hwaet	bridge
geong	quick
geolu	milk
taegl	yellow

Medieval scribes

The French Invade!

In 1066, William the Conqueror and the French invaded England. They brought scribes with them who began to alter OE spelling. For example words spelt in OE with a **c** at the start were spelt with **ch** and words spelt in OE with **sc** were spelt with **sh**. Can you spot any examples from the research you have just done?

DID YOU KNOW?

Medieval scribes got paid by the inch for what they wrote. So they added extra letters to the words!

The Printing Revolution

William Caxton brought printing to England with some odd results for spelling.

DID YOU KNOW?

Caxton used foreign spellings for some English words: *ghost* for *gost*.

Caxton wanted to save money, so he used the same letters for more than one sound! So **gh** is used in *cough* and *laugh* as well as *ghost*!

Caxton wasn't as careful as printers are today. Different spellings were used for the same word: *fellow, fellowe, felwe, felow*, for example.

The Pronunciation Revolution

For some reason, the pronunciation of words began to shift in the fifteenth century. However, whilst the pronunciation changed, the spellings remained much the same. This, to some extent, accounts for the unusual use of vowel symbols in our modern spelling.

Here's an example of how a sentence was probably pronounced before this change (or Great Vowel Shift, as it is sometimes known) took place:

> *And saw it is team noo to say hose narma is on the show and if the sarma fate can doe the daunce toneet that hath such farma aroond the toon.*

Here's what it sounds like in modern English:

> *And so it is time now to see whose name is on the shoe and if the same feet can do the dance tonight that has such fame around the town.*

Scholars Get It Wrong!

Many scholars in the reign of Elizabeth I thought that lots of English words should be spelt like Latin ones. So they added letters to words when they ought not to have done!

For example: *rime* became *rhyme*, *dette* became *debt* and *iland* became *island*.

The result was some rather odd spellings! There's no link between spelling and pronunciation in these cases.

Foreign Imports

English has imported lots of words from other languages, but has kept the foreign spellings. The pronunciation has been a source of disagreement sometimes, with the result that English spelling has added complications! You'll have a chance to look at this in one of the research projects later.

Do you think that the 'foreign' words should keep their original pronunciation or should they take on an English pronunciation? How do you pronounce words like *restaurant* or *reservoir*, for instance? Can you think of any more words from foreign sources that have shifting pronunciations?

You can work on your own, in pairs or in groups on any of these investigations into English spelling. The essential tool that you will need is a good dictionary. If you can get hold of an etymological dictionary (one that tells you about the origin of words), so much the better. The best dictionary in the language is the huge *Oxford English Dictionary*, but there are lots of other good ones available, including ones published by Longman, Collins or Chambers.

1   If you have access to a word processor, type in a passage of English from an earlier age and then run the spell-check through. Which words are highlighted by the spell-check? Does this tell you anything about how spelling has changed? Do you notice any patterns emerging?

2   You have already seen that one of the causes of irregularities in English spelling is that there are more sounds than letters in the alphabet (approximately forty-four to twenty-six). One of the results of this is that almost every letter in English has more than one pronunciation. For instance, the **s** in *house* and in *houses* is quite different. Say them aloud to yourself to prove it! See how many different pronunciations you can find for **g**, **c**, **a**, **x** and *z* by collecting a list of words that demonstrate each one. Are there any of these letters that have only one pronunciation? You could, of course, continue this investigation with all the letters in the alphabet.

3   Many of the words that have come into English from other European languages have affected our spelling. Sometimes we have just taken the foreign spelling, but have given the new 'English' word our own pronunciation (like *chauffeur* or *yacht*). Sometimes we have 'anglicized' the spelling (like *sherry* from the Spanish word *jerez*). Many of these words come from certain topic areas, like food or music. We have begun a chart that you should try to add to – there are lots of words that you could find.

Food and Drink

France	Italy	Germany	Spain	Russia	Others
omelette	pizza	sauerkraut	paella	borsch	whisky
blancmange	spaghetti	hamburger	sherry	vodka	pastrami

venison	tagliatelle	pretzl
veal		
pork		
sardine		

MUSIC		
piano	waltz	guitar
solo	glockenspeil	
crescendo		
concerto		

There are other topics that you could investigate: transport and travel, clothes, architecture, painting, for example.

4 If you have younger brothers and sisters or can go into a primary school, you could obtain examples of children's writing. You may even have some of your own work that you (or your parents) have kept. This is very useful research data, as you can use it to investigate children's spelling. Collect as much as you can, but to start you off, here's a short story written by a seven-year-old from Manchester, called Nicky. It's called *I Can't Wait till Crismas*.

once a boy called malcum coudent wait till crismas he was allways so ekcited and here's the story whie one day malcum coudent wait till crismas it was only one week till crismas on Monday he was playing with his next door neighbour and rolled his truk and it fell in a hoel that dad dug and it was very deep and so dark malcum wasent sad bucuse he coud get one at crismas. on tuesday he was playing on his own and by axedant broke his car and throw it away in the bin and he dident mind again becuse he coud get one on crismas on Wenesday, he was holding his toy aeroplane on the way to the Park and triped up and broke the aeroplane dont worry Ill get one on crismas on Thursday he as playing football and a dog poped the ball malcum did not mind ill get one at crismas on Friday he was playing crikit and took a fast blow at the ball with the bat and hit the ball so high he lost and broke the bat on

Saturday he was playing tenis and tryed to hit the ball and when he hit it it went throw the bat and lost that ball tow I dont mind said malcum. on Sunday he was playing chess and lost a peace he was not sad but you cant play chess with out a peace on crimas he got a truck a car a aeroplane a ball a crikit set and a tenis set tow and a good turkey dinner and a crismas puding.

These are some of the questions you could ask to help you investigate children's spelling:

a   What proportion of words are spelt incorrectly? People always seem to complain about spelling, but Nicky gets many words right in his story!

b   What types of word (e.g. nouns, verbs, adjectives, etc.) seem to give the writer the most trouble?

c   What causes the writer to make spelling mistakes? Here are some possible reasons:
   – spelling words as they sound;
   – omitting silent letters (*nocked*);
   – confusing different words with the same sound (*piece/peace*);
   – having single letters where they should be doubled (*tenis/tennis*).

What others can you find?

5   You'll need to consult a very good dictionary for this piece of research. Try to produce a chart that traces the changes in spelling of particular words over time. Here's an example of how *merry* has changed its spelling:

1200   *murie, murgre, murgore, mirie*
1300   *muri*
1400   *meri, myry, miry, mury*
1500   *mery, mirry, merry, merrie*
1600+   *merry*

Other words that you will find have changed their spelling quite a lot are *shield, round, bowl, comb, ear, jolly, toe(s), fight, fruit.*

DOUBLETS

This word games was invented by Lewis Carroll, of *Alice in Wonderland* fame. The aim is to turn one word into another by changing only one letter at a time. The snag is that each single change has to result in a new word. For instance, *pig* becomes *sty* in five moves like this:

```
P   I   G
W   I   G
W   A   G
W   A   Y
S   A   Y
S   T   Y
```

Try these. They can be done (honestly!)

NINE	to	FIVE	(two moves)
EAST	to	WEST	(three moves)
GIVE	to	TAKE	(four moves)
SHIP	to	BOAT	(five moves)
ROCK	to	ROLL	(six moves)

Chapter Three

ENGLISH WORLD-WIDE

DID YOU KNOW?

There are more students of English in China than there are people in the USA.

There are 168 national airlines in the world, and 157 of them use English to communicate with each other.

In earlier parts of the book, we've seen how English has changed. Changes are still taking place today, but on a world-wide scale.

A WORLD LANGUAGE?

English is spoken by more than 350 million people in the world as their first language; only Chinese is spoken by more than this. In over sixty countries, English has special status as an official language, and some 1,400 million people live in these countries. Facts like these suggest that English may well be on the way to becoming the world's language. On the map below you will see where in the world English is spoken as a mother tongue and/or as an official language and where it is an important foreign language.

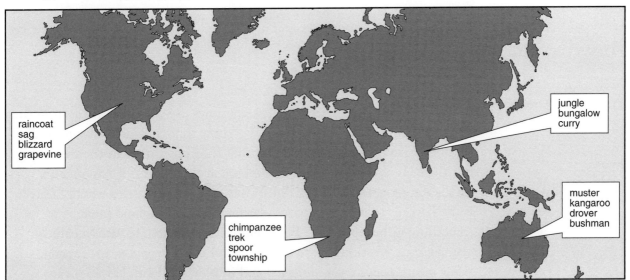

Some words adopted into English from other countries.

In Britian, we have special historical ties with some of the countries where English is spoken: India, Australia, the United States and South Africa, for example. It's not surprising, therefore, that many words that began life in these countries have become part of the language which we should perhaps call British English to distinguish it from Australian English or American English. Some of these words are also shown on the map.

Here is a list of some more words and expressions that come from these four countries (Australia, India, South Africa and USA) that are in common usage in British English. By using a good dictionary, try to decide where each word comes from.

cheetah	fan	phoney	boomerang	commuter
overland	publicity	verandah	briefcase	apartheid
airline	commando	nirvana	hangover	tinnie
zipper	radio	kookaburra	plonk (wine)	jodhpurs
juggernaut	teenager	concentration camp	stockman	ranch
barbie	checklist	laser	joyride	graveyard
yoga	gimmick	striptease	stunt	pundit

1 Which country seems to have supplied the most words? Why do you think that this is the case?

2 Were there any words that were easier to place than others? Why?

3 Were there any words that weren't in your dictionary? *Barbie*, for example? What enabled you to place them?

FALSE FRIENDS

We all know that Americans sometimes use different words from the British for the same thing. We know that they use *elevators* and not *lifts* to save climbing stairs and that they put things in the *trunk* and not the *boot* of the car. We'll be looking at this aspect of American English in more detail later. But in lots of other countries where English is used, words that have a particular meaning in England mean something rather different. For example, in Jamaica, to *stain* means *to taste sour*; in West Africa, *to take in* means *to get pregnant*; in Canada, *riding* means *political constituency*; and in New Zealand, *hurray* means *goodbye.* Here are some other examples of these false friends at work.

WORD	COUNTRY	MEANING
robot	South Africa	traffic lights
park	Australia	parking space
mind	Scotland	remember
station	Australia	farm
chop	Malaysia	rubber stamp
duty	East Africa	work
delight	Wales	interest
carpet	West Africa	linoleum
forget	East Africa	lose
smallboy	West Africa	servant
bioscope	South Africa	cinema
crib	New Zealand	cabin
bold	Ireland	naughty
dread	Jamaica	excellent
front up	Australia	turn up

Working in groups, discuss reasons for the difference in meaning in each case. For instance, the two words from West Africa may well tell us something about the way of life in that part of the world. Or think about how traffic lights operate. Would that explain the South African word? Then present your suggestions to the rest of the class.

DID YOU KNOW?

There are twice as many words in common use in English than in French.

Seventy-five percent of the world's mail is written in English.

WHY HAS ENGLISH BECOME A WORLD-WIDE LANGUAGE?

Up to the end of the sixteenth century, if you had travelled abroad, you would have heard very little English spoken. If you'd crossed the Atlantic, you might have heard a little Spanish, but in the main, you'd have heard one of the many native American languages. It would have been the same if you'd managed to reach Australia, South Africa or

India – all you would have heard would have been tribal languages. You wouldn't have even been able to call the countries by the names we know them by today. So why did English spread all over the world more than any other language? What does this tell us about the power of Britain and America over the last 400 years?

In the following list we've suggested sixteen reasons why English has come to be the dominant language in the world. Discuss them and decide what your group thinks is their order of importance.

1   Missionaries went out from Britain to try to convert native peoples to Christianity.

2   The USA is the centre of the world's film and TV industry.

3   Britain was a great colonial power in the eighteenth and nineteenth centuries and conquered many parts of the world.

4   The USA and West Indies had many slaves from Africa.

5   British and American pop music is the best in the world.

6   The USA was once a British colony.

7   Britain used to be the most powerful economic and trading nation in the world.

8   Overseas students come to Britain and the USA to be educated.

9   English is one of the most adaptable and easily learnt languages in the world.

10 Everyone wants to eat Big Macs, wear Levis and drink Coke.

11 British systems of education, government and religion were exported all over the world.

12 Some of the best authors in the world wrote in English: Shakespeare, Charles Dickens, Mark Twain and William Wordsworth, for example.

13 America is the most powerful nation in the world today.

14 Other languages are inferior to English.

15 New means of communication, such as fibre-optics, satellites and the Internet, have increased the use of English world-wide.

16 Because there is a great variety of languages and dialects in countries that used to be part of the British Empire, English is a ready-made means of widespread communication between people who speak these different languages.

Discussion Topic

Does the spread of English all over the world mean that people who speak English are more powerful and influential than those who don't?

To help you in your discussion, here are some comments from foreign learners of English, which are quoted in *The Cambridge Encyclopedia of Language.*

'When I finish learn English, my pay as secretary will be increase by nearly ten times.' (*Egyptian trainee secretary*)

'My company plans big deals with Arabic world. None of us speak Arabic, and they do not know Japanese. All our plans and meetings are in English.' (*Japanese businessman*)

'After I learned English, I felt I was in touch with the international world for the very first time.' (*Nigerian teacher*)

'If I want to keep up to date with the latest techniques and products, I must certainly maintain my English very strongly.' (*Indian doctor*)

DID YOU KNOW?

Eighty per cent of the information stored in the world's computers is in English.

English is the main language for international business, medicine, diplomacy, pop-music and advertising.

AMERICAN ENGLISH

In this section, we're going to look at American English and we'll see whether we agree or disagree with this declaration made in 1923:

The official language of the State of Illinois shall be known hereafter as the American language, and not as the English language.

American English is probably the most influential English in the world today, thanks to American power in lots of important areas: entertainment, communication systems and business, for example. Certainly, many people think that it is the liveliest and most exciting English of all. Journalist Henry Porter thinks 'there is an imaginative force in American English which has not been active in the spoken word here for two and a half centuries.' However, some people disagree:

Americans invent all sorts of new nouns and verbs and make words that shouldn't be. (Prince Charles, 1995)

We must act now to ensure that English – and that to my way of thinking means English English – maintains its position as the world language. (Prince Charles, 1995)

The words and accent are perfectly disgusting, and there can be no doubt that such [American] films are an evil influence on our language. (Conservative MP, 1938)

If there is a more hideous language on the face of the earth than the American form of English, I should like to know what it is. (Member of the House of Lords, 1978)

What do you think?

IS IT ENGLISH?

Here are eight short extracts from *American*. We'd like you to read through them carefully and note down anything that seems to you unacceptable as British English. For instance, it might be the spelling of *program* or the expression *stay home*.

1   If you can't be king of the hill, you may as well stay home. So put the 1992 Toyota 4WD Xtracab at your command and you'll rule over most any domain. (Advert for Toyota Trucks)

2 I would like to thank the Giants . . . for possibly having a part in my acceptance to Notre Dame, my first choice college. I knew I wanted to attend ND more than any other school. My admissions counselor told me how important the application essays were. (Letter in the San Francisco Giants Baseball magazine)

3 Say you're sitting in Candlestick Park, patiently waiting for a ballgame to begin. All of a sudden, people start leading cows onto the field. And players start milking them. Honestly, this is happening. Then, the veteran players make the rookies participate in a cow-chip tossing contest. Too much to handle. Do you start to wonder what was in the polish dog you just ate? (San Francisco Giants Baseball magazine)

4 Team up with Avis for great low rates on quality GM and other fine cars. Rates and cars are subject to availability. Rates are nondiscountable and blackout periods may apply (Avis Car Rental advert)

5 At age eight Michael taught himself to play guitar and then in school took up the trumpet and stuck with both instruments through high school. As a senior he finally got hold of his uncle's fiddle but did not get his own until he was 21. Michael majored in English literature at LSU. (CD insert for Hot Chili Mama)

6 Best Western can provide you with accommodations close to business appointments, airports and city center locations worldwide.

For an explanation of our corporate program please dial . . . (Best Western Travel Guide, 1988)

7 There are many publications available at the Bookstore about various parts of the art collection, and the visitor is referred to these books and catalogs for detailed information about individual works of art. (The Huntington Art gallery, San Marino, California)

8 Walking across interment sections is not permitted except to visit interment spaces. Take extreme care to avoid memorial tablets, lawn vases and sprinkler heads. (Guide to Forest Lawn Cemetery, Hollywood)

When you have noted the differences, sort them into these categories that we have suggested. We've filled in some to get you on your way.

DIFFERENT SPELLING	DIFFERENT GRAMMAR	WORDS/EXPRESSIONS NOT USED IN BRITISH ENGLISH
center	my acceptance to	interment space
program	accommodations	

We say *potayto*, you say *potarto*

Can you speak 'American'? We all think that we can imitate American accents and that we could play the gangster in the film when he says 'You dirty rat!' But is it that easy? British and American pronunciation *does* differ. Try reading aloud the following passage, which we've put together, though we admit it's rather an artificial one! There are at least fifteen words in it that Americans pronounce differently than we do. We've shown you which they are.

Can't *you give me the* **address** *of the* **leisure** *centre in* **Derby?** *The hotel* **clerk** *couldn't answer my* **inquiry** *and I've got to get there by the fastest* **route** *if I'm to keep to* **schedule** *to see the* **ballet** *at* **half** *eight. And another thing! All I've had to eat today has been a* **tomato** *and* **herb** *omelette made with* **margarine** *not* **butter** *and a* **banana** *fritter.*

It's very easy to hear American speech in Britain. All you have to do is to watch television and you'll hear US politicians, sports stars and entertainers being interviewed, and of course you'll be able to see lots of American films and TV shows. For this investigation, you'll need to watch TV for some time. As you do so, note down all the words that Americans pronounce differently and then compare them with your own pronunciation. Here's a chart that you could copy to help you record your findings. You will have to invent a way of spelling that reflects the pronunciations. We've given you a start.

WORD	AMERICAN PRONUNCIATION	BRITISH PRONUNCIATION
letter	ledder	letter

Norfolk	Norfolk	Norferk
vase	vaze	varse
lever	levver	leever

Do I make myself clear?

Perhaps the strongest argument for saying that there's 'American' and there's 'English' is that the vocabulary of the two nations differs quite a lot. In fact, it's estimated that there are over 4,000 words that are used differently. Lots of room for confusion and mistakes here! There's a story told by author Bill Bryson of an American lady recently arrived in England, who opened her front door to find three men there informing her that they were her dustmen. 'But I do my own dusting,' she said!

In the following list, there are twenty-five American words together with their British equivalents. The only trouble is that they need matching up! See how many of the twenty-five you know.

AMERICAN	AMERICAN	ENGLISH	ENGLISH
cookie	biscuit	jam	ugly
barf	gas	skiver	undertaker
pacifier	realtor	queue	petrol
teeter-totter	mortician	braces	hairslide
sheers	homely	autumn	biscuit
jelly	jello	jug	footpath
pitcher	overpass	scone	garden
ground-round	trunk	estate agent	net curtains
hood	suspenders	baby's dummy	vomit
yard	line	flyover	jelly
faucet	sidewalk	see-saw	boot (of car)
fall	barrette	minced beef	bonnet (of car)
goldbricker		tap	

To work out your score, turn to the end of the chapter.

25   You are American (or have cheated!)

19–24   You spend too much time watching *Dallas*, *NYPD Blue*, *LA Law* and *The Cosby Show*.

12–18   You wear Levis, drink Coke and eat Big Macs at the same time as liking fish and chips, soccer and Tizer!

6–11   You are British and proud of it! Damn Yankees!

0–5   You have no TV, don't read, watch films or listen to music.
       What *do* you do?

As a final test of your ability in American English, here are ten English
words for which you have to find the American equivalent:

postman	flat (where you live)
draughts	fridge
advertising hoarding	caretaker
car bumper	drawing pin
nappy	railway

DID YOU KNOW?

Britain earns £2 billion from English language services, making it our sixth largest
export earner.

Half a million visitors to Britain every year study English in our schools and colleges.

AUSTRALIAN

We're all quite familiar with the Australian accent, thanks to TV
programmes like *Neighbours* – or we think we are! Here's a
conversation in 'Australian', spelt as Australians would pronounce it. Can
you understand what the conversation is about? Try saying it out loud.

– *Sell semmitches air?*

– *Emeny jiwant?*

– *Gimme utter martyr and an airman pickle. Emma chisit?*

– *Nimepen slidy.*

In his amusing book *Let's Talk Strine*, Afferbeck Lauder tries to show by
using the ordinary letters of the alphabet how Australians pronounce
English. He enjoys surprising and baffling the reader by running words
together or breaking them up, and by using words which contain the
sounds he needs but which have quite different meanings from the words
the speakers have in mind. For instance:

stewnce = students   *tiger* = take a   *sander's lape* = sound asleep

a gloria sty = a glorious day   *share* = shower   *hip ride* = hit parade

Translate the next ten Strine (Australian) words and expressions into English.

We've given non-Australians a bit of help!

1 *rise-up lides* (found in the bathroom)

2 *spin-ear mitch* (look-alike)

3 *split nair dyke* (aspirin needed)

4 *fitwer smeeide* (I advise you to . .)

5 *sag rapes* (sets your teeth on edge)

6 *airpsly fair billis* (really great)

7 *egg jelly* (to tell the truth)

8 *fipes-, temps-, corpse-,* and *harps-two* (look at the clock)　　　,

9 *scettin lairder* (not as quiet as it was)

10 *garbler mince* (not long)

And for the more advanced student of Strine (or those who never miss an episode of *Neighbours*!), here are more examples to translate, but this time without any clues!

1 – *Laze and gem. It gives me grape leisure . . .*

2 – *Thenk smite.*
 – *Dimension.*

3 – *I gunga din, the door slokt.*
 – *Hancher gotcher key?*
 – *Air, buttit spoultered on the inside. Car more, nopt-nit.*

4 – *Sarn's calmer nairt. Scona beer gloria sty. Mine jute still scold zephyr. Cheat was cold la snite.*

JAMAICAN ENGLISH

There are many 'Englishes' in the world, as we have seen, and we are not going to have time to look at every one of them. But Jamaican English – or British Black English as it is sometimes known – has quite a special place for us because not only can you hear it used in Jamaica and the Caribbean, but it's easy to hear in the British Isles as well. You may well use it yourself at home or with friends. Even if you don't, you're quite likely to have heard it from other people at school or used by reggae or rap singers. The main reason that it is found in Britain is because many people emigrated from the West Indies in the 1950s and their children and grandchildren live here as British citizens, but still at times like to use Black English. Of course British Black English has changed a little from its Jamaican roots, but does share many similarities.

We'll look at two aspects of it that are different from Standard English, before looking at an example.

Grammar

1   Black English doesn't always indicate plural endings on nouns. *Five tree* or *seven book* rather than *five trees* or *seven books*.

2   Black English doesn't use 's to show possession. *This girl dress* or *that boy brother* rather than *this girl's dress* or *that boy's brother*.

3   Black English sometimes misses out *is* in sentences like *he very good-looking* or *she going to Tesco* rather than *he is very good-looking* or *she is going to Tesco*.

4   Questions are sometimes different. Black English will have *Who this is?* or *Why you are going?* not *Who is this?* or *Why are you going?*

There are many other grammatical differences between Black and Standard English, and you'll be able to spot some of these in the extract.

Vocabulary

Here are just some of the vocabulary differences. Try to collect as many more as you can.

BLACK ENGLISH	STANDARD ENGLISH
backra	boss, white person
bounce	to jostle
buck	to stub your toe
dunny	money
extra	boastful
hard ears	stubborn, disobedient
kwabs	companions
peelhead	bald man
spar	friend

A word of caution about vocabulary. Some of it changes so fast and goes out of fashion so quickly that some of these words may be out of date by the time you use this book. That's why it's important to do your own research on language and, in this case, collect as many Black English words as you can. Here's an example of British Black English, produced by a writer who is proud of her language. This is the opening of a story, *Ballad for You*, written by Jennifer Johnson, who has lived all her life in Brixton, the centre of 'Black London'. The speaker is introducing five college friends.

There is five gal I want to tell you 'bout. Dem lick head from different part of a London; but is one t'ing dough, dem is one an' di same but individual in every sense. Mek a tek dem one by one.

Lightening hail from Guyana an' is a soul-head. Before she buck head wid dem addah gal she couldn't chat a word a bad English; now she pass GCSE ina it. Why dem call she Lightening is because when dem sit down ina corner a chat people business, she always miss everyt'ing an' confuse di issue. She live up ina bush Lan', according to di addah four gal, Thornton Heath, Surrey.

Chalice come from Guyana too, but she come jus' like a Jamaican to di addah gal dem. She can chat bad an' love a gossip. She better dan any newspaper or radio. She live a North London an', out a all a dem, dis is di Top Bitch.

Nex' come Charlie. She is a bwoy in every sense but wid looks. She love a trouble an' always deh in di thick of it. She hate all di soul-head dem, excep' fi Lightening, because she t'ink dem mad. Trouble is she noh know seh she mad too! I mean if you a goh mash up six chair an' set dem a fire ina de middle of di common room dat pack up wid people, somet'ing wrong some where: I wonder is soh all Peckham people stay?

Granny Roach is jus' four feet an' mish-mash, but, bwoy, she have di biggest mout' in di world. She live a Dulwich an' fi she family is di only black family pan di road. She is an only chile (thank God, him know whey him a dhu) but, Lord, she have dem whites pan she road undah manners. An' fi a person no bigger dan a cockroach, she have many people walking in fear, because of her mout'.

Squeakey is di last pan di list. She live right pan di Front Line a Brixton. So everybody kinda cagey 'bout she (so we wont seh no more 'bout she for mi noh want any contract out pan mi life).

What differences are there between the way this extract is written and Standard English? Remember that some of the spellings that look strange are there to show how the narrator would pronounce the words. Can you spot any differences in either the grammar or in the words and expressions that she uses?

WORD COUNT

In this game, each letter of the alphabet is given a number value. So A = 1, B = 2, C = 3, D = 4 . . . X = 24, Y = 25, Z = 26. The aim of the game is to see who can get the highest score for a two-letter word, a three-letter word, a four-letter word and so on. Words must appear in the dictionary, so you wouldn't score 104 for ZZZZ! You are only allowed to consult the dictionary after selecting your word.

Answers for page 33

AMERICAN	ENGLISH
cookie	biscuit
barf	vomit
pacifier	baby's dummy
teeter-totter	see-saw
sheers	net curtains
jelly	jam
pitcher	jug
ground round	minced beef
biscuit	scone
hood	bonnet
gas	petrol
realtor	estate agent
mortician	undertaker
homely	ugly
jello	jam
overpass	flyover
trunk	boot
suspenders	braces
yard	garden
faucet	tap
fall	autumn
goldbricker	skiver
line	queue
sidewalk	footpath
barrette	hairslide

Chapter Four

STANDARD ENGLISH, ACCENT AND DIALECT

STANDARD ENGLISH

'The lads done well, and we're dead chuffed to have rolled 'em over.'

'The team played well, and we are delighted to have beaten the opposition.'

The second statement is expressed in Standard English; the first one is not. Why not? Look at a) choice of words and b) grammar. The first sentence uses:

- slang, such as *dead chuffed* and *rolled 'em over*;
- *done well* rather than the standard forms of the verb in the past tense: *did well* or *have done well*.

The following five sentences contain 'non-standard' uses of English. Decide what are the non-standard forms of English and what their equivalents would be in Standard English.

1 I'll just lay down for a bit and have a kip.
2 I were gobsmacked when she give us the brush off.
3 She's much more kinder than our last Principal.
4 I has to sup me cup of char quick.
5 He's the chap what did the robbery.

Most people would probably agree that Standard English:

- is the variety of English (both spoken and written) which is most widely recognised and readily understood by the majority of users of the language;

- avoids vocabulary and grammar found only in regional varieties of the language;

- follows fairly uniform rules in its grammar, vocabulary and spelling;
- carries prestige and is felt by many to be 'correct' English.

Here are a number of specific comments and examples which relate to the use of Standard English. Decide in each case which of the four general qualities of Standard English listed above they illustrate.

It is Standard English that is taught in textbooks written for foreign learners of the language.

Standard English is a form in which a child is a child (not a bairn) and in which a church is called a church (not a kirk).

There are a very few variations in the spelling of Standard English (for example, judgement/judgment and verbs that can end -ise or -ize), but in general, its spelling is uniform.

A businessman from Tyneside, giving directions over the phone to a customer from London who wants to visit his factory, begins, 'It's a geatt five mile . . .' and then says, 'It's a good five miles from Newcastle.'

If someone who was learning English asked us what the expression nobbut meant, we would probably use Standard English as a point of reference to explain that it was a northern dialect form of nobody but.

In oral assessment for GCSE, pupils are expected to show that they can use Standard English.

The pilots of nearly all the world's airlines speak Standard English when they are communicating with air-traffic controllers.

It was decided by the BBC to use Standard English in the early days of broadcasting.

Consider the following two points which relate to the history of the development of Standard English.

Standard English was originally based on the kind of English used by educated people from the region bounded by London, Oxford and Cambridge. Why should this form of English have been taken as the 'standard', rather than that of, say, the south-west or the north-west?

Why was development of Standard English given impetus by the following?

• the steady growth of the printing of books in the sixteenth and seventeenth centuries;
• the increasing movement of people around the British Isles in the nineteenth century as they changed jobs and moved into new areas;
• the establishment of a common educational system for all people in Britain;
• the spread of English as an international language;
• developments in broadcasting and mass communication.

Standard English is the language in which (we hope) most of this book is written; it is the language you will hear from the newscaster in the television news. What if we were to write, 'Hey, all you kids out there, get an earful of this . . .'? Or if the newscaster were to begin, 'Oh, my brothers and sisters, yous gonna get yisselves some real hot news from yer main man . . '? Most people would feel that the wrong tone was being adopted and, in the second case, some might not understand what was meant.

> **W**orking in pairs, decide in which of the following situations you would expect to find Standard English used.
>
> 1 A letter your parents write to the head of your school, asking for permission for you to miss the last week of term so that you can begin a foreign holiday early.
>
> 2 A lawyer summing up a case in a court of law.
>
> 3 An answer in a GCSE examination in which you have been asked to summarise the main points made in a newspaper article.
>
> 4 A speech made at school assembly by the representative of a charity who is explaining the main aims of her organisation.

Now outline four situations in which you would *not* expect Standard English to be used. In what kind of situation could you not be sure whether Standard English would be used? Why might this be so?

Non-standard English can add character!

When they are writing a story in the first-person – that is, using a character to tell his or her own story – writers often use a non-standard form of English, if this happens to be the way in which the character concerned would tell the story. This technique is a very good way of creating a sense of the speaker's character. Here, for instance, is the way Mark Twain makes Huck Finn, an imaginative but ill-educated American boy, begin his story.

> *You don't know about me, without you have read a book by the name of* The Adventures of Tom Sawyer, *but that ain't no matter. That book was made by Mr Mark Twain, and he told the truth, mainly. There was things which he stretched, but he mainly told the truth. That is nothing. I never seen anybody but lied, one time or another, without it was Aunt Polly, or the widow, or maybe Mary. Aunt Polly – Tom's Aunt Polly, she is – and Mary, and the Widow Douglas, is all told about in that book – which is mostly a true book; with some stretchers, as I said before.*

Write a version of this passage in Standard English. You will have to change a number of words and sort out some of Huck Finn's sentence construction. For example, your version might begin: 'You will not know about my character, unless you have read a book entitled . . .' What, if anything, has been lost by writing this passage in Standard English?

What sort of a boy does Huck now seem to be in the revised version? (And why is this so?)

Spelling

The system of spelling is one aspect of Standard English about which there are few disagreements. Spelling is certainly something that you will need to pay attention to in the following letter which we want you to re-write in an appropriate form of Standard English and then explain why such a form would be suitable for this letter.

6.5.96   12 Brook Rd, Anytown
                                                    AT4 3NW

mister Enyam – I should of wrote you sooner but Ive bin bisy. me mates have bin naggin me to get in tuch. we has this band its calld Bonky Squirrel and we was wondrin if youd be interested in usin us for a gig at yer club. which we rekon is ~~grate~~ grate!!! should we post you a tape of the kinda stuff we do, weve played at our locul youff club and evryone sez we was grate, dont worry we would not want to much bred, any nite wowd do us. write as soon as pos or give us a bell if that soots yours truley hopefuly –
                        Sammy (drums)
                              ⌣(◠‿◠)

ACCENT

Accent refers to the way words are pronounced. Everybody has an accent. So far, we have discussed some ways in which Standard English affects vocabulary and grammar. Many people think that Standard English also requires a certain sort of accent, but this is not so. It can be spoken in a whole variety of accents, which will usually reflect the region of the country from which the speaker comes. For instance, a speaker from the north will probably pronounce a short **a** in words such as *bath* and *pass* (*pass* here will rhyme with *mass*) as opposed to the longer **a** sound of a southern speaker, who will pronounce *bath* as if there were an **r** in the spelling (*barth*). Again unlike someone from the south,

Wot toime his the next troine fer 'Ammersmith?

Due now.

Course Oi dawn't now stoopid, or Oi wouldn't be harskin' yer!

a northern speaker's pronunciation of the vowel **u** in words such as *us* or *bus* may come close to the sound of the vowel in the standard pronunciation of *buzz*. Of course, these are general differences; an expert in **phonetics** (that is, the study of the sound of speech) would be able to distinguish a wide variety of different vowel sounds in a range of, say, Lancashire or Yorkshire accents.

Because we are usually comfortable with what is familiar, some people may find the accents of those who come from other parts of the country strange or even amusing. There is no logical reason for this, though sometimes the differences between accents can lead to misunderstanding. For example, what is the reason for the comic misunderstanding in the conversation that takes place in the cartoon?

Harriet has a Cockney accent, as the unusual way of recording her speech tries to show. Try speaking her words as you think they would sound. Now, work in pairs and try to convince your partner that you can produce the following accents:

1 Lancashire;

2 Birmingham;

3 Newcastle;

4 Somerset.

You might begin by trying to say, in the appropriate accent, 'The team played well, and we are delighted to have beaten the opposition'. Then move on to see how many other regional accents you can manage to reproduce.

1

If accent is dictated principally by where you live, which of the following factors may also influence it? If you think any of these factors are important, be prepared to say why.

- the kind of school you went to
- the level of education you achieved
- the social class you belong to
- the climate where you live
- how much money you earn
- the job you have

- the friends you mix with
- how intelligent you are
- your general state of health
- whether you want to impress people
- whether you have travelled widely
- whether you are a man or woman
- the way your parents speak
- the influence of people on TV you admire
- how ambitious you are
- whether you read books a lot
- whether you are young or old
- whether you are aware of what accent you have

Are there any other influences not on this list?

2

Why is it common experience for people who move to a new part of the country to find, particularly if they are young, that their accent gradually changes? What do you think is the reason for this kind of change?

3

Are there any circumstances in which you are aware of changing or modifying your accent? If so, in what kind of circumstances and to achieve what kind of effect?

Talkin' posh

Received Pronunciation (often abbreviated to RP) is still felt by some people to be the ideal form of spoken English. This accent is based on that of upper-class speakers in the south-east of England and, until fairly recently, many people who wished to get on in their jobs or in society changed their local accents to RP. That is why Received Pronunciation should not be thought of as belonging to any one region of the country: a lawyer who was born in Newcastle, a public schoolboy from Dundee who went to school in Edinburgh or a university lecturer who once had a broad Cornish drawl might all speak in an RP accent. If you spoke RP, people once believed you must be powerful, important and have lots of status. RP was generally the accent you would have heard on the BBC from the early days of broadcasting in the 1920s. If you are in any doubt what it sounds like in one of its purest forms, listen to the Queen's speech on Christmas Day or watch some old British black-and-white films from the 1940s on television.

Once upon a time RP might have been the necessary passport to success in education, politics and the professions (for example, medicine and law), but today most educated people speak in a manner which mixes RP with modified forms of their regional accent. Indeed, to many people today, by a kind of reverse snobbery, an RP accent may be associated with a 'stuck-up' or affected manner. Possibly television and popular entertainment are important influences here. In the 'Swinging Sixties', for example, a northern, and particularly a Liverpudlian accent, became fashionable, and a lot of people who had a 'public-school accent' did their best to lose it as quickly as possible. In the 1980s, many people commented on the rise of 'Estuary English' – a modified form of a London accent which had spread far beyond the capital as a result of the scattering of thousands of Londoners and the effect of long-distance commuting. The influence of a whole string of media personalities, such as Ben Elton and Jonathan Ross, also contributed to the popularity of an informal style of 'London-speak'.

Our attitude to regional accents is tied up with various social assumptions and prejudices. We may feel that certain accents are 'sloppy' and that others sound melodious or grating. Some accents may be felt to carry a sense of greater authority and status than others. But how do we arrive at these judgements? What factors will tend to make us prefer one regional accent to another? The following piece of research should lead to some answers and help to define the attitudes people have to a range of regional accents.

First, you will need to make a recording of a range of regional accents from speakers on the radio and television. You might include examples of the accents of the north-east, Liverpool, Birmingham, London and the south-west. Make sure that there is one example of a speaker who has the regional accent of your own area and one 'neutral' accent which is virtually free of any distinct regional sound.

When you have your various voices on tape, prepare a questionnaire, preferably to be answered by another class which is not currently studying this topic. (Ask your teacher to play the recording to the 'test group' and to collect their answers.) Remember, we are essentially interested in finding out what *attitudes* people have towards a range of regional accents, so after you have asked whether the listeners can identify the part of the country a particular speaker comes from, we would suggest the following kinds of questions:

1   If you were looking for somebody to read the news, which speaker would you choose?

2   Which speaker would you employ to do a 'voice-over' for a television commercial to sell the following: a family car; a brand of bread?

3   Which speaker would you least trust? For example, which speaker sounds like the kind of person you would not buy a second-hand car from?

The first question is designed to assess the measure of authority people associate with a certain accent. What do you think we are trying to establish with our second and third questions? Now, think up some further questions of your own.

When you have the answers to your questionnaire, write a report on the conclusions you would draw from your survey.

DIALECT

Many people think that accent and dialect are the same thing. They are not. An accent refers to the way words are pronounced (we have already heard how different accents may colour the pronunciation of a standard form of English when we experimented with the way 'The team played well . . . etc, might be spoken by someone from, say Somerset or Birmingham). Dialect, however, refers to forms of English which do not merely sound different, but which show differences from Standard English in vocabulary, grammar and word order. Well into the twentieth century, each part of the country had its own clearly defined dialect of English which could only be fully understood by the people of that region.

The next passage we shall look at shows the way Emily Brontë in *Wuthering Heights* (1847) records the speech of one of her characters,

Joseph in *Wuthering Heights* (1939).

[Actor: Leo G. Caroll]

Joseph, as he greets an unwelcome visitor. We may assume that Joseph speaks in the dialect that Emily Brontë would have been familiar with, having grown up in that part of the Yorkshire Moors around Haworth and Keighley. We come from the other side of the Pennines, and we have to confess that we find parts of Joseph's speech very difficult to understand. Can you work out the general gist of what he is saying? Pick out examples of dialect words (words which are peculiar to Joseph's region of Yorkshire).

Vinegar-faced Joseph projected his head from a round window in the barn.

'Whet are ye for?' he shouted. 'T' maister's dahn i' t' fowld. Goa rahned by th' end ut' laith, if yah went tuh spake tull him.'

'Is there nobody inside to open the door?' I hallooed, responsively.

'They's nobbut t' missis; and shoo'll nut oppen 't and ye mak yer flaysome dins till neeght.'

'Why? Cannot you tell her who I am, eh, Joseph?'

'Nor-ne me! Aw'll hae noa hend wi't,' muttered the head vanishing.

laith = barn   flaysome = frightening

Dialect is still alive today. In Lancashire, for example, some speakers may still call an alley that runs between houses a *ginnel*; in Leicester, the same thing is referred to in dialect as a *snicket*. And do you always call a bread roll a *bread roll*? Are you familiar with any of the following words for the same thing? *Barm cake* (Lancashire), *bap* (Leicester), *batch* (Coventry). Do you know any other word for this item of food?

Perhaps you think you use no dialect words. Consider, however, the words you use in everyday conversation for:

a) mother
b) yes
c) no
d) thank you
e) nothing

For a group of students from Manchester, the words they used for those listed above, in conversations with family and with close friends, were: a) *mam*, b) *aye*, c) *nay*, d) *ta*, e) *nowt*. The students concerned were happy to use such words – they 'had a warmth about them' said one.

In fact, like many words preserved in dialect, *nowt* has ancient roots. In this case, the word goes back to the Anglo-Saxon *nōwiht*, which meant *nothing* well over a thousand years ago. The same Anglo-Saxon word gives us *nought* meaning *zero*, which is a perfectly 'respectable' piece of Standard English, and *naught* (also meaning *nothing*) which would now be seen as old-fashioned or literary English, in an expression such as 'He set his foes at naught'. Another example of northern dialect preserving an older meaning would be the use of the word *starve*. In Anglo-Saxon, *steorfan* meant *to die*; in Middle English, the word came to mean *to die of cold* or *from hunger*. In northern dialects, speakers will still say today, 'I'm starving!' when they mean, not that they are hungry, but that they are feeling very cold.

Collect some words of dialect that are peculiar to your own part of the country. Even if you do not know any yourself, you may find that by listening to older people, or by questioning relatives, you can pick up some examples. Some questions along the following lines should be a good starting point. Ask about:

1   terms of praise and criticism – words for 'good' and 'bad';

2   words to do with the weather, for example, words for drizzle or a hot day;

3   exclamations or mild swear words;

4   words connected with the behaviour of children; for example, words for being naughty, well-behaved or brightly intelligent;

5   terms that describe certain kinds of food, such as bread, cakes or different kinds of meat;

6   words for greeting people or saying farewell (other terms for 'hello' and 'goodbye').

Some questions for general discussion

- If dialect words have been dying out of the language for some time, why do you think this is so? Is this trend something to regret?

- Many people are aware that, while they have an excellent command of Standard English, in certain circumstances they

> slip into the kind of 'local' speech or dialect they grew up with. In what circumstances do you think this might tend to happen? Is there any advantage for a person who can command both Standard English and a local variety of the language?
> - What would be the disadvantages for a speaker who could *not* move from a regional dialect to Standard English?
> - What is the difference between dialect and slang?

So far we have been considering the vocabulary of dialects; in our initial definition of dialect, however, we noted that a dialect also affects the grammatical structures of language. It should be emphasised that, while some of these dialect forms will sound strange or 'incorrect' to those who are familiar only with Standard English, they are perfectly consistent usages of English within the dialect. Decide in which of the following categories you would place each of the expressions listed below.

a   I use (or used to use) this expression.

b   I do not use this expression, but I know people who do.

c   This is a Standard English expression.

d   This would not be allowed in any form of English.

1   My clothes need washed.
2   I'm here, aren't I?
3   He like her a lot.
4   She can't sing that, too.
5   He did it himself.
6   She wouldn't do that, would 'er?
7   I'll come over; I might could do it.
8   I'll stay while ten o'clock.
9   The jeans as he got were clean.
10   She ain't coming.
11   I'm not going there; it's nearly five mile.
12   I says to him.
13   He drove that fast, he crashed.
14   There's men who's got nay sense.
15   You can cut your hand off that glass.

In the following table, we give you some widely used examples of dialect or non-standard forms of English in which the grammar is different from that of Standard English. In each case, write down the equivalent form in Standard English. We have done the first one for you.

DIALECT/NON-STANDARD	STANDARD
I have took his pen.	I have taken his pen.
I knowed him was there.	
Give us them books.	
There is three guys in the room.	
She ran out the door.	
Dave come home last week.	
We ain't going to work.	
They was faster than us.	
I'll lend the lawn mower off him.	
I'll learn you to do that!	
He boxes very crafty.	
I didn't get no pay last week.	
He's very friendly-like.	
He seen thee hisself.	
Us'll be at the game Saturday.	
I'm off out, me.	
She didn't say nothing wrong.	
He was just stood there on his tod.	
He was sat there laughing.	
He's the baddest crook.	
He's crazy is Bill.	

A GOOD PRESCRIPTION?

We began this section with an attempt to define Standard English. It would be wrong to give the impression that Standard English is frozen into some fixed form. In fact, there are various levels of formality and informality within Standard English. Moreover, as language is living and constantly changing, what is considered 'standard' alters as the language develops, though there are some people who would like to try to stop language changing. However, a word which was once considered to be slang becomes an accepted usage; a construction which one generation considered 'sloppy' is used quite happily by the next. In Chapter 6, you will find a number of examples of this process.

A **prescriptive** approach to language means one which lays down definite rules about what is correct and what is incorrect. As many people believe they know a lot about language, there are a great number of people who are inclined to offer prescriptions. Sometimes the motive for the approach is to attempt to preserve English in what is claimed to be a kind of 'ideal', or at least superior, form. Of course, we must make sure that whatever we say or write is expressed as clearly as possible; however, there is a danger that in 'laying down the law', we either become over-concerned with very minor matters (possibly at the expense of ignoring more serious issues) or we express as a 'rule' what is no more than a prejudice or a matter of personal taste.

GENERAL DISCUSSION POINTS

1 In France, L'Académie Française issues edicts about what is 'good' and 'bad' French. For instance, in recent years the Academy has attempted to ban words which have come into French from English – expressions such as *le weekend*. Do you think Great Britain would benefit from the setting up of a similar organisation?

2 Give your opinion on the three statements below:

'The use of English is in decline because pupils are no longer taught grammar in schools and they are allowed to get away with using sloppy speech.'

'Instead of prescriptive rules about English, we ought to concentrate on descriptive ones: they should be rules based on how people actually talk and write, and not on how they ought to do so.'

'There is no such thing as Standard English; it is wiser to think in terms of the usage of a number of varieties of English in particular situations and for particular purposes.'

26

Twenty-six is a crucial number for word gamers, and the reason should be obvious! Here are three games that are connected by the fact that there are twenty-six letters in the alphabet.

1   Try to invent a sentence that contains all twenty-six letters (a **pangram**). The most famous examples of such a sentence is *The quick brown fox jumps over the lazy dog* which has thirty-five letters. Of course, it's not too difficult to make a pangram if you invent a fairly long sentence with lots of duplication of letters. The point of the game is to see who can come up with the sentence that has the fewest letters. Twenty-six is almost impossible! We couldn't do it!

2   Write a sentence of twenty-six words, each word beginning with the consecutive letter of the alphabet. The problem is that the sentence must make some sort of sense. To prove that it can be done, here are two examples:

   a A born coward, David eventually found great happiness in joyfully kicking loud mouthed nitwits, openly picking quarrels, rightly saying that unkindness vied with Xavier's youthful zeal.

   b A bronzed cowboy, dancing elegantly for grand hotels in Jersey, knitting lovely mittens nicely on prettily quilted rubber shoes, thought untrained vets would X-ray your zebra. (quoted by David Crystal)

3   Can you complete this dialogue? Note how each speaker begins with a consecutive letter of the alphabet.

A   Are you going to the club tonight?

B   But of course.

A   Can I have a lift, then?

B   Do you need to ask?

A   Exactly what I hoped you'd say.

B   Fine.

A   Go and get ready.

B   How should I be dressed?

A   I don't really care.

B   Jeans, OK?

A   Keep those on. What make are they?

B   Levi's.

Chapter Five

LANGUAGE AND POWER

Have you ever noticed how full of rules and regulations people's lives are? At school there's always someone telling you when that work has to be finished or when you can or can't speak. At home, it's probably the same: 'Do this!' or 'Don't do that!' And it's not just young people who find this – adults, too, find their lives subject to similar pressures.

In this section, we're going to look at how language can be used to exercise power in people's lives. We'll see that it's not just a matter of being told what we must and must not do; often, it's much more subtle than that. We might, for instance, be persuaded by a powerful advertisement to wear a particular brand of clothing, a very powerful and effective speaker might persuade us to lead our lives in certain ways, or we might have our opinions moulded or changed by what we read. Life is full of 'experts', 'manipulators' and 'people who know best'!

Here are some short examples in which language is used to demonstrate power in various ways. Discuss each one with your partner and try to identify:

a   what type of writing it is and any possible source for it (some are very obvious);

b   how the writer is trying to affect us (our behaviour, conduct, attitude, for example).

We've made some suggestions about the first three to help you.

1 Here are some short examples in which language is used to demonstrate power in various ways. Discuss each one with your partner and try to identify. . .

a   Instructions from a school textbook on language. Which one?

b   Telling school students what to do in the hope that they'll understand more about how language is designed to influence and affect people.

2 *When a boy's everything you need – hunky, funny, cute 'n' kind – heaven doesn't seem that far away.*

a Extract from a teenage girl's magazine, like *Just 17*.

b Implying that a particular type of boy (*hunky* etc.) is the key to a girl's happiness.

3 Instructions to Candidates
Answer **three** questions in all:
one question from **Section A**
one question from **Section B**
one question from **Section C**

You must write the title of your project on the front of your answer book before attempting your first question.

a Part of the front cover of a GCSE examination paper.

b Indicating that the Exam Board has the power to fail you, if you don't follow these instructions.

4 *Do not give to children under twelve years unless on doctor's advice. Do not exceed the stated dose.*

5 *I promise to pay the bearer on demand the sum of five pounds.*

6 *No smoking. Penalty £50 maximum.*

7 *Don't miss this chance to buy this vest by our favourite designers, Pauli and Sara. It normally costs £24, but readers can buy it at an exclusive price of £14.*

8 Review:
Out on video this week:
Judge Dredd (15)
The Flintstones (U)

9 *Bolton Wanderers F.C.*
Where appropriate this ticket is for the seat stated only. Please take your position at least 30 minutes prior to kick-off. This ticket is not transferable.

10 *Patrons are advised not to leave valuables in their cars.*

11 ERRORS IN THE USE OF WORDS
Words wrongly used:
Alright – there is no such word. The correct form is all right, *and its opposite is* all wrong.

12 *No entry.*

13 *The scooter must be driven only by the person who signed the contract. When someone else drives the scooter and has an accident, the insurance company does not cover that accident.*

14 *Thank you for not smoking.*

15 *Fly our new Boeing 777 for just £777.*

16 *I told you to be back before midnight. It's nearly one o'clock already!*

17 *We strive to deliver services which meet our customers' needs and expectations. Our standards are set out in the Passengers' Charter available from mainline stations or by post from our Customer Relations Manager whose address is shown below.*

18 *Nothing in this magazine may be reproduced in whole or in part without the written permission of the publishers.*

19 *This voucher should be carefully preserved since it will be accepted by the Inland Revenue as evidence of entitlement to Tax Credit.*

20 *Who do you think you're talking to?*

We are constantly bombarded with signs and notices that give us commands or make requests of us. In the list of extracts you have just worked on, there were two examples of such signs. Collect as many other examples as you can. You'll find them in school, public buildings or as you walk down the street: no smoking signs, no trespassing signs, litter signs, signs encouraging you to be quiet and so on. For each sign, we want you to indicate:

1 where it was situated;

2 what the tone of sign was (bullying, polite, stern, humorous, gentle, friendly, threatening, etc.);

3 whether you think the sign would achieve its desired effect;

4 whether you think there is any connection between the tone, the setting and the effectiveness of the sign.

ACRONYMS

An **acronym** is an abbreviation formed from the first letters of a series of words (like NATO for **N**orth **A**tlantic **T**reaty **O**rganisation). English has lots of words like this, and new ones are forever entering the language. Of course, many people don't know what most of them mean because they are not experts in a particular area. Computer freaks, for example, talk knowledgeably about RAM, ROM and WYSIWYG. Do you know what these acronyms mean? To understand acronyms and use them in situations where not everyone will understand them can be a display of power: 'I'm an expert, but you're not!' Throughout this section of the book, you'll find acronym quizzes: we give you an acronym together with three possible meanings. Two are false; you have to decide which of the suggestions is the correct one. You'll soon become an acronym expert.

SALT

a) Strategic Arms Limitation Treaty

b) Stop All Late Trains

c) Society of American Language Translators

ASH

a) Action on Smoking and Health

b) Australian Superhighway

c) Alcoholics Self-Help

QUIET
NO NOISE!

NO
TRESPASSING

POWER RELATIONSHIPS

The way we use language, both when we speak and when we write, changes according to the status or power of the person we are addressing. You probably don't speak to your teacher in the same way as you speak to your friends! But, as we'll see, it can be a little more complex than that.

Power in relationships is likely to depend on four factors:

1   Age: whether one speaker (or writer) is older than another.

2   Knowledge: whether one speaker (or writer) is an 'expert' in the subject under discussion.

3   Status: whether one speaker (or writer) is felt, or feels him/herself, to be superior in status to another.

4   Physical power: whether one speaker is bigger or stronger than another.

Here is a selection of situations that will involve conversation. Discuss them with a partner and, for each one, decide whether either of the speakers is more powerful than the other and, if you think that one is more powerful, which of the four factors we have indicated above (age/knowledge/status/physical power) gives him or her this power. Remember, more than one factor may be operating at once.

1   You are being interviewed for a Saturday job at a local shoe shop by the manager.

2   You are explaining to your father how to use the new family computer.

3   Your brother is interviewing an employee at a local firm about his role within the company.

4   Your science teacher is introducing a difficult new topic to the class.

5   Your science teacher is discussing the lesson with a visiting inspector.

6   You and your boy/girlfriend are deciding which film to see at the local multiplex cinema.

7   Your grandmother is talking to her councillor because the local library is to be closed.

8 You are talking to your younger brother/sister who has rightly accused you of 'borrowing' a T-shirt without asking.

9 You are talking to the manager of the local shoe shop because one of the heels on a pair of shoes you bought last week has broken off.

10 You are explaining to your English teacher why you haven't handed in your homework.

11 You are speaking to your English teacher about your favourite football team/band/hobby/film.

12 You are discussing these questions with someone else from your class.

You will need three people for this activity. Choose one of the situations you have been discussing. Two of you should act out the parts in a short piece of improvisation. The third member of the group should be the observer and note down any features of the language used that indicate that one of the speakers is possibly more powerful than the other. For example, you might look at:

- who begins the conversation;
- the way the speakers address each other;
- who speaks most;
- the tone(s) of voice used by the speakers;
- whether any specialised or technical language is used;
- how frequently questions or commands are used;
- who ends the conversation and how this is done.

There are likely to be other features of the conversation you notice. The observer should then report back to the other two members of the group on the features of the conversation that showed either that one speaker was more powerful or that the power was more evenly divided.

See if the features remain the same in every conversation. Choose another one from our list (or invent one of your own, such as a visit to the doctor's). This time, have a different observer.

IMF

a) Indian Metal Foundry
b) Independent Miners'
        Foundation
c) International Monetary
        Fund

The Language of the Law

One of the situations in which power can be most clearly seen is in court. Courts can be frightening places for people unused to them; the procedures, the emphasis on incessant questioning and confrontation and the language used can make many people feel powerless.

Here's a short extract from a Scottish court case in which the defence lawyer is questioning a witness, Martin Neevy. Discuss how the lawyer uses language to try to maintain power over the witness.

LAWYER According to you, Mr Neevy, this ill-feeling, this grudge on Mr Robertson's part towards you, stemmed from an incident months previously when you had done something to a gate. He wanted you to repair a gate?

NEEVY Yes.

LAWYER Is that right? What happened to this gate?

NEEVY Er, I accidentally bumped it slightly with, er, the rear of my car.

LAWYER The rear of your car. Hmm. Did anything happen to you as a result of driving your car that day?

NEEVY [pause] No.

LAWYER Did the police come to see you?

NEEVY No. I can't remember 'em s-seeing me, no.

LAWYER You can't remember whether they came to see you or not?

NEEVY I don't think they did, no.

LAWYER Is that because the police have been to see you so many times, Mr Neevy, that you can't remember what they were up to see you about, one incident as compared to another incident?

NEEVY That's not true, no.

LAWYER And you know very well that the reason why there is ill-feeling between you and Mr Robertson is that you believe Mr Robertson shopped you to the police at the time you ran into his garden gate, and the police claimed that you were driving with no insurance. Isn't that right?

NEEVY [pause] No, it's not right.

LAWYER   So nothing like that happened at all?

NEEVY   I was prosecuted . . . possibly a week or so later, I believe.

LAWYER   What for?

NEEVY   For having no insurance on the car.

LAWYER   You put two and two together, Mr Neevy, and made five and suspected Mr Robertson of having shopped you to the police for driving a car without insurance.

NEEVY   That's not true. It's not what I thought, no.

WHO
a) Worldwide Housewives Organisation
b) World Health Organisation
c) West Highland Office

What did you call me?

One of the ways in which we can signal power and status in our relationships is by the names and titles we use when we speak to each other. It would be rather unusual if you always addressed your mother as *Mrs Smith*. Nor would Dr Andrew Smith expect a policeman who had stopped him for speeding to say, 'Would you mind, dear, if I saw your driving licence?' We choose **address terms**, as you probably realised from your improvisations, according to the age, status and the nature of our relationship to other people. Most of us are addressed in different ways throughout the day.

Here's a thumbnail profile of Dr Andrew Smith:

Dr Andrew Smith, aged 38, local GP, married to Pauline (35), a part-time primary teacher, two children: Michael (10), Zoe (4).

1   These are some of the ways in which he is addressed. For each one of the terms, suggest who might have addressed him in this way and in what circumstances.

Dr Smith / Dr Andrew Smith / sir / darling / Dad / Daddy / Andy / Andrew / Smith / you / mate / Mr Smith / stupid bugger / Doctor / Smithy

2   What address terms can you suggest might be used to other members of the Smith family and in what circumstances?

OED

a) Overhead Electricity
          Distribution
b) Oxford English
          Dictionary
c) Oil Exploration
          Department

It's possible to address people in different ways:

- we can use their title (T): Mr, Mrs, Dr, Professor;
- we can use their first name (FN): Paul, Angela, Uzma;
- we can use their last name (LN): Jones, Smith, Patel;
- we can use a word that shows respect for the person addressed: sir, madam, my lord;
- we can use a nickname: Smithy;
- we can use a combination of these: Mr John Smith;
- we can use nothing at all.

Keep a record for a period of time (a day, a week) of the address terms used by you and to you. You could use a table like this:

Situation	Address term you used	Address term used to you
You/doctor's receptionist	none	Love
You/doctor	Doctor	Miss Smith
You/maths teacher	Mrs Jones	Paula

Look at this rather extreme example of power relationship at work in a conversation. It's taking place between a white policeman and a black doctor on a public street in the USA.

POLICEMAN	What's your name, boy?
DR POUSSAINT	Doctor Poussaint. I'm a physician.
POLICEMAN	What's your first name, boy?
DR POUSSAINT	Alvin.

Dr Poussaint later reported that this conversation caused him 'profound humiliation'. Discuss why you think he felt this way. After your discussion, you might find the following comments helpful.

- The policeman used what is an insulting term for an adult: *boy*.
- The policeman is white and so used *boy* because he believes whites are superior to blacks.
- He continued to use it, even when he discovered the black man is a doctor. People usually give doctors a great deal of respect.
- He wanted to know Dr Poussaint's first name, as if he were speaking to a child.

Language and prejudice

This 'conversation' between the policeman and Dr Poussaint reminds us that there are other reasons for power differences between people, and these also show themselves in the ways we use language. They are the ones based on prejudice.

You've already looked briefly at one of these, racial prejudice, and we'll examine another in more depth in Chapter 9, **Language and Gender**. Here, we'll look briefly at a third: prejudice based on class.

Are U U?

The playwright, George Bernard Shaw once wrote:

> *It is impossible for an Englishman to open his mouth without making some other Englishman despise him.*

It's true that almost everything and anything about the way we use language can indicate class: the names people give their children, the accents we have and the words we use. In the 1950s, Nancy Mitford invented the expressions **U** and **non-U** for upper and non-upper class and she claimed that certain words for the same thing would be used only by U people and others by non-U people. So, for instance, it would be U to say *bike* and non-U to say *cycle*.

Here are some other word-pairs which are supposed to indicate what social class the speaker is. Discuss them and see if you can decide which is the 'posher'.

vegetables	greens
house	home
ill	sick
mad	mental
toilet paper	lavatory paper
rich	wealthy
dinner (midday meal)	lunch (midday meal)
dinner (evening meal)	tea (evening meal)
drawing room	lounge
pardon?	what?
settee	sofa
lavatory	toilet
rugby	rugger
champers	champagne

Can you think of any other pairs to add to this list?

There are plenty of soap-operas on TV that have mainly working-class characters: *Coronation Street* and *EastEnders* are probably the two most popular at the moment. The scriptwriters of these programmes try to have their characters speak as realistically as possible. Some of the vocabulary used will certainly be non-U!

Watch a number of these programmes and note down the vocabulary used which seems to you to indicate that the character is meant to be working class. You'll need to indicate who spoke the words (age, sex and race are important here) and in what sort of situation the words were used (family row, pub chat, shopping, for example).

Some questions to ask:

1 How accurate are the writers in depicting working-class vocabulary?
2 Are there any differences between the vocabulary used in different programmes?
3 Did all the characters in a programme use the same type of vocabulary?

Write a short scene in the form of a script for TV, radio or film that uses some of the language you have observed. Of course, there are lots of other programmes to research. You don't have to confine yourself to soaps.

Power of persuasion

We all know that advertisements are powerful and can persuade us to buy things we didn't know we wanted or can change our minds about particular issues. We'll be looking more closely at the language of adverts in Chapter 13, but there are ways other than adverts that can be used to influence us, perhaps without our realizing it. Magazines aimed at teenagers and young adults are a good example. Here are some short extracts from one issue of a magazine aimed at teenage girls. We've put comments next to each extract to indicate how we think the writers hope to influence their readers.

1	Fame! I wanna life forever! Eight ways to be a supermodel.	Filling readers' heads with unattainable dreams.
2	Wanna zoom ahead of other earthlings this summer? Go for a look that's fresh and futuristic without looking like you've dropped in from Mars! Space babes get stars for cool make-up with a soft shine – glossy silver eye shadow, jet-black eyeliner, white hot nails and shimmery lips.	Buy and wear this type of make-up and cosmetics and you'll be very fashionable. No one wants to be unfashionable.
3	Last year we saw models stalking the cat-walks with ruby-red lips, and this year is no different. But watch out – red fever is on the rampage!	This year's fashion is to wear red lipstick. It must be good as top models wear it. More red lipstick will be sold!
4	Aries: if you were waiting for him to make a move after he told a friend he fancied you, then you're going to have to wait. That doesn't mean he's got the huff, just that he's taking his time.	Girls are passive: they wait for boys to make the first move. This assumes that all girls must have a boyfriend.

Here are some more examples, this time without comment. What comments would you make about them?

5	Don't call me weird but . . . 'I can't get a boyfriend!'
6	Classic denim is easy to wear and looks cool any time, any place, on anyone. Here's how to look electric in blue! A denim jacket tied round the waist is a great way to hide your rear end and still look cool.
7	Man of the month – Leo. How to spot him: he's the lively, outgoing, charismatic guy with the dazzling smile. How to attract him: be enthusiastic about everything and shower him with flattery and affection.

Choose a magazine with which you are familiar. Select four or five short extracts that seem to you to be attempting to influence the readers in some way or other. Present these extracts to the rest of the class in a similar way to the one above.

ACRONYMS – THE FINAL WORD

Finally, some acronyms without any suggested meanings. See if you can supply your own meanings for them! Anything suitable considered! These acronyms really do exist.

CAB	CUP
FIDO	CAR
RAN	PEP
DOE	MOD
NEB	SQUID

REBUS

A **rebus** is a word puzzle that uses letters of the alphabet plus numbers, symbols and pictures to make a word or a sentence. This is one of the most famous ones, together with its translation.

YY U R	Too wise you are
YY U B	Too wise you be
I C U R	I see you are
YY 4 me	Too wise for me

Here are some more for you to puzzle out. We've given you clues to make life a bit easier but not for the first two, as rock fans should have no difficulty with these.

1	XTC	
2	INXS	
3	B 10	defeated
4	URAQT	very pretty
5	XLNC	ambassador
6	SX	in England
7	EGNC	lots of islands here near Greece
8	KT 8 A ∏ 4 T	she enjoyed the tart
9	XQQ	sorry
10	U C A K9 B4 U	where's Fido?

Chapter Six

SLANG

If your teacher said to you 'Shut yer gob!', you would probably be shocked. If you addressed your teacher in the same way, you might be told, 'How dare you talk to me like that!' The classroom is still a fairly formal place, and language of this kind would be unusual. You may also feel that 'Shut yer gob! is an example of slang that sounds rather old-fashioned.

Slang is language which is not an accepted part of Standard English. It is normally spoken rather than written, it is often recently invented and it is constantly changing. Slang is often felt to be inappropriate in 'polite' or formal use. Some people might claim that slang is merely 'sloppy' language, and so it may be when it is used in the wrong context, or over-used to the point of becoming clichéd. Yet when the expression 'Chill out!' (meaning 'Relax!' or 'Take it easy!') was first used, it must have seemed quite vivid. And the American hospital doctor who coined the phrase 'crispy critter' to refer to a patient suffering from severe burns was certainly inventive, even though he or she could have been accused of sick humour.

Slang certainly shows how speakers of a language can invent and discard words very rapidly. Many slang words and expressions have a brief shelf-life in the language. The use of *gob* for *mouth* quickly died out, and when it is used now, it sounds dated. (The word did return again briefly in the term *gobsmacked* which, in the 1980s, was northern slang meaning *totally shocked*.) However, some words may begin their life as slang and later be accepted as Standard English, having become 'perfectly respectable'. For example, consider the word *slum* in the cartoon at the beginning of this section. This word was once used, in the early nineteenth century, by only a small group of tramps; today, it is a perfectly acceptable term to describe a deprived, run-down area of a city. Words such as *mob*, *sham*, *jazz* and *bully* were once slang, but most people would regard them now as part of Standard English. (In contrast, the use of the word *quid* for *a pound* was slang when its use was first recorded in 1688, and it is still slang now.)

Dear sir . . . I must protest!

When people claim a piece of slang is simply sloppy speech, they may be putting forward what is really no more than a personal or social attitude towards language. What is slang for one person is somebody else's normal way of speaking. The definition of exactly which words are slang and which ones are not may be a difficult business, but people often express dogmatic views on the subject. The following letter, written to the BBC Complaints Department, is not at all unusual.

Dear Sir,

I am fed up with the kind of language we hear on the BBC these days. Only today, on the News at One on Radio Four, I heard the following two examples. The interviewer said to the Prime Minister, 'Lots of people feel the government is clapped out.' And then he followed it up just a moment later by asking, 'Does this mean we're into a whole new ball game?' Well I ask you! I nearly had a fit! Such language shows a lack of respect, not only for the Prime Minister, but for the audience of the programme. And the second quote is not even English slang – it's American!

How can we expect our young people to use English correctly when they are set such a bad example by people who should know better? I hope you will do something to remedy the kind of slovenly speech we hear all too often on radio and television.

Yours faithfully,
A. Enyam.

This letter was broadcast over the air. Do you agree with Mr Enyam? Write a letter to the BBC either supporting or rejecting his views. Use examples of speech that you have heard on radio or television.

isten to the news on television or the radio (or ask your teacher to
bring a recording into the classroom) and list all the words you
consider to be slang. Make a note of whether the slang is spoken
by the newsreader or occurs in an interview. (Why is this distinction
important?) Compare your list of words with other people's lists and
see whether you can agree on what is slang and what is not.

MAKE IT EASY ON YOURSELF

One of the major reasons for change in many areas of language is the
desire to simplify. This certainly applies to the kind of slang words
which first appear as shortened forms of some longer word. Over a period
of time, the abbreviated word often become the accepted form, and the
original word begins to sound long-winded. 'I'm going to the *zoological
gardens*' certainly sounds a bit of a mouthful! Most people today simply
go to the *zoo*. Again, it is likely you would refer to a lesson in the *gym*
rather than in the *gymnasium*.

In the case of each of the following words find out, using a dictionary if
you do not already know, the original, longer form of the word.

1 petrol	11 piano	21 lunch
2 telly	12 bus	22 navvy
3 phone	13 fridge	23 stats
4 taxi	14 car	24 lab
5 cab	15 fan	25 advert
6 plane	16 pub	26 pop (music)
7 pants	17 bike	27 bookie
8 bra	18 cello	28 sub (three meanings)
9 mike	19 hi-fi	29 vac (two meanings)
10 burger	20 exam	30 perm (two meanings)

Would you say that all the above words have stopped being slang?

MAKING SLANG

In this section, we are going to look at three other common ways in which slang words come into existence.

1 Prefixes and suffixes

Many slang words are formed by the addition of **prefixes** or **suffixes**. Prefixes are groups of letters that are added to the beginning of existing words; suffixes are groups of words tacked on to their endings. For example, the prefix *mega* has come to mean *very great*. This generates such expressions as *megabucks* (a very large sum of money – a *buck* is, of course, American slang for a *dollar*) and *megascore* (a very high score). The suffix *wise*, meaning *concerning* or *as regards*, gives birth to words such as *health-wise*.

In the three columns below are some suffixes followed by a short definition of what the suffix usually means. See how many slang expressions you can add to the list. To start you off, we have given you a few examples.

-ie (type of person)	-able (capable of being . .)	-ist (holding a certain position or beliefs)
foodie	huggable	sexist
groupie	danceable	ageist
hubbie	fanciable	televangelist
veggie		
yuppie		

2 Compound expressions

Some slang terms are formed by joining two words together to produce a new word or combination of words. We call this a **compound expression**. Quite often, some kind of comparison is involved when we do this. For example, a *couch potato* describes an inactive person; the idea is that the person referred to spends such a great amount of time sitting, probably watching television, that he or she might be imagined 'to have taken root'. What is the idea behind the term *coffin nail* as a slang term for a

cigarette? What do you think is the origin of the terms *pub crawl*
(meaning a drunken evening spent in several pubs) or *meat market* (for a
certain kind of club or disco)?

Imagine that, having given the meaning of the following expressions to a
foreign visitor, you are asked to explain how the terms came into
existence.

1 money-spinner

2 winkle pickers

3 heart throb

4 male chauvinist pig

5 chattering classes

6 monkey suit

7 bovver boy

8 culture vulture

9 birthday suit

10 gobsmacked

11 stage-struck

12 slime ball

Can you think of any other examples of slang compound words? And now a challenge! Make up your own compound slang expressions that would describe each of the following:

1   the kind of person who 'always knows best';
2   somebody who is obsessed by computers and their software;
3   a strict person;
4   a meal that is bound to give you indigestion;
5   a long and boring lesson.

3 Creative slang

Inventing new slang can be very creative. G. K. Chesterton, an English novelist, said that 'The one stream of poetry which is constantly flowing is slang. Every day, some nameless poet weaves some fine tracery of popular language.' A lot of slang is rather more down-to-earth than the weaving of 'some fine tracery' suggests, but Chesterton is surely right in pointing to the way in which slang is often produced by **metaphor** (comparing one thing with another). The gangster term, *a wooden overcoat* (a coffin) certainly creates a very striking image!

The trouble with even the most creative slang is that it soon becomes a cliché and loses its power to strike us. For instance, the term *dead from the neck up* to describe a stupid person has been used so often that it has become a 'frozen metaphor'; the expression has lost the power of its insulting comparison. Read the following list of slang words that have been used to describe stupid people and try to work out the comparison which inspired each of the terms:

dummy	spongecake
peabrain	featherbrain
numskull	prathead
cabbage	birdbrain
sawdust brain	zombie
silly billy	mophead
nutcase	dickhead

All of these insults are rather worn out, so draw up your own list of words that you use to describe someone you think is a fool. Get your teacher to write the words you come up with on the board; we think you will be surprised how long the list is! When you have compiled your list, decide how many of the words are based on a comparison. Carry out the same procedure in connections with words to describe:

a   the police;

b   money;

c   clothes;

d   parts of the body.

WHERE DO THESE WORDS COME FROM?

Slang words come from a wide range of sources. In the next activity, you will need to use a good dictionary and reference books to find out where these slang words came from. Choose one or two words from the list, and then report back to the rest of your class about what you have found out.

yob (hooligan)

grotty (nasty, unattractive)

bumf (useless paperwork)

booze (alcoholic drink)

bobby (policeman)

mugger (thief who robs by threats of violence in the street)

switched-on (alert, intelligent)

wimp (timid person)

grub (food)

nark (police informer)

posh (upper-class; smart)

waffle (meaningless padding out of writing or speech)

ginormous (extremely large)

gazumped (to be outbid by somebody after you have agreed the price for buying a house)

boob (blunder)

whodunit (crime novel)

wangle (to use a devious method to achieve one's aims)

manky (dirty or decayed)

cad (old-fashioned slang for a man who does not behave in a gentlemanly manner

recce (preliminary inspection)

shrink (psychiatrist)

mush (face)

WHO'S SLANGING WHOSE SLANG?

Pool your knowledge by working in groups of four or five on the following activity.

A **Thesaurus** lists synonyms (words or expressions that come close to the meaning of the same idea). All the words and phrases below are synonyms for being drunk.

a peg too low   a sheet (or three sheets) to the wind   bevvied up blind   blotto   boozed-up   bottled   canned   corked   foxed groggy   half-seas-over   in one's cups   legless   lit up   loaded lushy   one over the eight   mellow   muzzy   paralytic   pickled pie-eyed   pissed   pixillated   plastered   raddled   rat-arsed shickered   sloshed   smashed   soaked   soused   sozzled squiffy   stewed   stinking   stoned   tanked up   tight   tiddly tipsy   top-heavy   under the table   well-oiled   whiffled.

Divide these expressions for being drunk into three categories:

a   in everyday use today;

b   used by some speakers, but old-fashioned;

c   not in use today.

Are there any other slang expressions for getting drunk that you could add to the list?

Now, still working in groups, imagine that you are compiling your own *Thesaurus of Modern Slang* that lists synonyms for the following ideas or conditions:

a   feeling very unhappy;

b   losing your temper;

c   praising something that is greatly admired;

d   criticising something that is strongly disliked.

DATING SLANG

One of the aims of the previous exercise was to underline how quickly slang becomes 'dated' or old-fashioned. It is very unlikely that you would use the term *a peg too low* or *three sheets to the wind* to describe someone who was drunk, but your grandparents may have done so.

A man who was once in the Royal Air Force told a group of other ex-RAF men this story. Can you work out what he said?

> *The erk who was D I-ing the kite didn't have a clue, and his oppo told him he'd better get weaving or Chiefy would tear a large strip off him. Then Corp came up in a flat spin with the gen that Groupy wanted the kit in an hour. The erk muttered that he wasn't carrying the can for anybody, that he wasn't Joe, that he couldn't care less about scrambled eggs, and that anyway he was browned off.*

The following definitions of some of the slang might help you.

erk: an air craftsman (most junior rank in the RAF)

kite: aircraft

oppo: operational officer (person in immediate charge)

Chiefy: commanding officer

tear a large strip off: reprimand severely

Corp: the corporal (a rank under a sergeant)

a flat spin: state of confused excitement

gen: information; news

carrying the can: taking responsibility or blame

scrambled eggs: a high-ranking officer (derived from the gold embroidery on the peak of the officer's cap)

1 At roughly what period of history do you think this slang would be spoken?
2 Do you get the general idea of what is being said? Try to summarise as much as you understand of this statement in 'plain English'.
3 Make a list of slang words from this extract which in your opinion would be (a) probably limited to the RAF at the period in question and (b) examples of slang that would be readily understood by most speakers of English.
4 Are there any slang words in the extract that you might hear spoken today?

EIGHTIES-SPEAK

The slang words listed below were all in fairly wide use in the 1980s. How many can you define? How many have continued their life in the language, as far as your use or experience of it is concerned?

brill	toyboy	dream ticket
hip hop	yuppie	wets
glitterati	bottom line	walkabout
yo	loony left	yomping
young fogey	brat pack	freebie
yardie	right on	fanzine
bimbo	thirtysomething	lager lout
loadsamoney	handbagging	wrinkly

Make your own list of some current slang – words that you believe have come into the language fairly recently. Some expressions may spring immediately to mind. A look through some 'teenage' magazines on subjects such as fashion or popular music will quickly add to your collection.

THE LANGUAGE OF THE TRIBE

Slang may be restricted to people of the same age. An older person, for example, might still describe someone who has been drinking as being *in his cups*, but you would not use the term. Alternatively, slang may be confined to one area of the country: do the terms *sarnie* or *butty* for a sandwich mean anything to you? The use of slang is also determined by social class. What background and age would someone be who used the word *preggers* for *pregnant*? (What other slang terms can you think of for *being pregnant*; and what do they tell us about the people who use them?)

Slang tends to flourish particularly well among groups of people with a lot in common, such as, for example, members of the armed services, young people who go to clubs that cater for a special kind of music or dancing, people in prison, computer hackers, drug addicts, rock musicians, workers who do the same job or players of a particular sport.

(What purpose does slang serve for those who use it in such groups?)

As a young person, you are probably involved in developing, or at least passing on, a constantly changing vocabulary of slang words. When you do so, you are claiming your own kind of language and marking it out as the specific possession of the group – or 'gang' – who are its users. Whilst you are at school, you belong to at least one important group of slang users. Some of this slang may be in general use among all students of your age; some of it may be unique to your school.

The following list of slang is a selection of words in current use in one school in Manchester. We would like you to go through the list and decide in the case of each word whether you recognise its meaning and whether you would use the word yourself. Work in pairs on this exercise and then compare notes with the rest of your class to discover how much agreement there is in your response to these words.

Slang Term	Definition	Understood by you	Used by you
sprog	pupil in the first year of the school	Yes/No	Yes/No
bogs	lavatories	Yes/No	Yes/No
butty bar	cafeteria where sandwiches and drinks are served	Yes/No	Yes/No
deef	prefect (derived from 'defect'?)	Yes/No	Yes/No
doss	as a verb, 'to do no work', as a noun 'something which requires no effort'	Yes/No	Yes/No
skive	to get out of work or to miss a lesson	Yes/No	Yes/No
greaser	person who 'sucks up' to a teacher	Yes/No	Yes/No
bod	a 'swot', someone who is over-studious	Yes/No	Yes/No

sorted	'That's fine', 'No problem'	Yes/No	Yes/No
babes	the first-year sports teams	Yes/No	Yes/No
raz(z)	rush, do some thing quickly	Yes/No	Yes/No

Now work out your own list of the slang that is current in your school. Imagine that you are presenting it to some new pupil or teacher in the school. Start by thinking, for instance, of words used to describe school subjects, meals, punishment, routine activities, sports or the different areas of the school. Is there any slang which is confined to one section of the school – to girls or boys, or to younger or older students?

SUBJECT/SITUATION

The 'rightness' of the use of any particular piece of slang depends on the context – the situation in which you find yourself. To whom are you speaking? How well do you know that person?

Each of the twelve sentences below begins with some direct speech. Give your opinion of the kind of person you think might have spoken these words and the situation in which the words might have been used. For instance, in the first example, we think the words might have been spoken by somebody in authority – maybe a somewhat old-fashioned schoolteacher who was once in the armed services. Perhaps the situation is that he (we think *chaps* is used only by men. Are we right?) is telling some young pupils to report to him to tidy up the mess in a classroom. It would be difficult to imagine the words spoken by a teenager to a friend, except as a kind of joke that involved acting a part.

Work in pairs, and when you have finished your answers, compare notes to see whether you agree with the rest of your class about the nature of the speaker and situation.

1 *Right chaps, I want the whole place ship-shape in two ticks . . .*

2 The old bag was barking last night – she's grounded me for a week just 'cos I wasn't in by twelve.

3 Most screws in this nick are bent.

4 Trueman, on a plumb track, could not produce any lift from a length, and his away-swinger was all over the show.

5 Lend me a little of the readies and I'll stand you some slap-up nosh the next time I'm in funds.

6 Honey chile, you reckon it cute to mosey downtown in that getup?

7 Even with a bullish economy, the kind of sleaze attaching to so many members of his cabinet means that the Prime Minister cannot rule out the emergence of a stalking horse.

8 That sad alkie tosser Joe's got right pissed again.

9 For a super-whoopin'-cruisin'-jumpin'-gnomy-puffin'-eatin'-drinkin'-sides-a-splittin' day, come to Flamingo Land between Pickering and Malton.

10 Just a quick cut and then scrunch it – I want to look drop-dead-gorgeous tonight.

11 OK man, so this cat wants to sit in? I'll take the head. Cherokee changes, and he blows the first six choruses – last two stop-time for the bridge.

12 This here's your main man who's gonna get you jiving, hiving and diving to this blast from the past – just beat the beat of this olden goldie.

SO WHY DO WE USE SLANG?

The list below is a summary of some of the reasons given by Eric Partridge, (*Slang: Today and Yesterday*, Routledge & Kegan Paul, 1933), a writer on language, to account for why we use slang:

• to show wit and inventiveness;

• to avoid expressions that have been used too often;

• to add directness and a striking quality to our speech;

• to reduce seriousness;

• to produce a feeling of close contact with another person;

• to show we belong to a particular group;

• to exclude others by the use of a private language;

• for the fun of it!

Now look back at the speakers and situations you have visualised when you were considering the snatches of speech in the previous section. In each case, which are the *relevant* reasons from the list given above for the use of slang? (More than one of the reasons may apply in many cases.) Are there are reasons *not* included in the list that you think are relevant?

SLANG IN WRITTEN LANGUAGE

A pupil writes in an essay, 'I am crazy about hang-gliding' or 'Romeo is crazy about Juliet'. In each case, the teacher has crossed out *crazy about* and written in the margin 'Avoid slang in formal work'. Is the teacher right, in your opinion?

To help you define the role slang may have in the written language, consider the two following extracts from the work of modern novelists.

A

After my siesta, I felt a little better, and I clambered quite gamely from the back seat to the front, only pausing to disentangle my ripped trouser-leg from the handbrake. Then I drove myself home – from Pimlico to Portobello in my purple Fiasco. Now my Fiasco, it's a beautiful machine, a vintage-style coupé with oodles of dash and heft and twang. The Fiasco, it's my pride and joy. Acting like a pal, I lend the motor to Alec Llewellyn while I'm in New York. And what do I return to? An igloo of parking-tickets and birdcrap, with ripped spare, a bad, new grinding noise, and every single gauge resignedly flashing. What's the guy been doing to my great, my incomparable Fiasco? It feels as though he's been living in it, subletting it. Some people, they've got no class.[1]

The passage is written in the first person (the 'I' tells the story). Does this make a difference to the kind of language Martin Amis uses here? Locate some examples of slang in the extract. What do we learn from the slang about the character in question? (Take into account the fact that slang is mingled in this extract with some language – *resignedly* and *incomparable*, for instance – of a different nature.)

B

There was me, that is Alex, and my three droogs, that is Pete, Georgie and Dim, Dim being really dim, and we sat in the Korova Milkbar making up our rassoodocks what to do with the evening, a flip dark chill winter bastard though dry. The Korova Milkbar was a milk-plus mesto, and you may, O my brothers, have forgotten what these mestos were like, things changing so skorry these days and everybody very quick to forget, newspapers not being read much neither. Well, what they sold there was milk plus something else. They had no licence for selling liquor, but there was no law yet against prodding some of the new veshches which they used to put into the old moloko, so you could peet it with vellocet or synthemesc or drencrom or one or two other veshches which would give you a nice quiet horrowshow fifteen minutes admiring Bog And All his Holy Angels and Saints in your left shoe with lights bursting all over your mozg.[2]

This passage is the opening of Anthony Burgess's novel, set in an imaginary future; the main character, Alex, tells the story in a kind of slang – it is called 'Nadsat' which is an invention of Burgess's that mixes English rhyming slang (see page 95) with elements of Russian. Why do you think Burgess felt the need to invent a special kind of language for this story? What is gained by doing so? Are there any disadvantages?

By looking at the context and using a little imagination, most readers find it fairly easy to work out what the slang words mean in *A Clockwork Orange*. Write a glossary which defines the following:

droogs	veshches
rassoodocks	moloko
mesto	peet
skorry	horrowshow
prodding	mozg

[1]Martin Amis: *Money* (1984) [2]Anthony Burgess: *A Clockwork Orange* (1962)

BOOKENDS

The letters L-I-G-H-T are at the centre of a word. Add **en** to the beginning and the end of them and you'll get **enlighten**. Now you have a go at making common words by adding the same letters before and after these following letters. Plurals not allowed! We've given you a few clues as to the meaning of the words.

_ MOEB _
(primitive life)

_ _ SUL _ _
(for diabetics)

_ _ PHABETIC _ _
(letter order)

_ _ GIB _ _
(easy reading)

_ _ AS _ _
(rubber)

_ _ _ ERGRO _ _ _
(city transport)

_ MERIC _
(country)

_ _ AT _ _
(eloquent speaker)

_ _ _ ROW _ _ _
(toenail problem)

_ _ RON _ _
(city)

_ _ CO _ _
(Spy's skill)

_ HI _
(US State)

_ _ UR _ _
(worship centre)

Chapter Seven

JARGON

THE POSITIVE SIDE

Jargon has a good and a bad side; two distinct meanings are reflected in its dictionary definitions. We shall begin with the positive one:

> *jargon* **1**. *The specialised or technical language concerned with a particular subject, profession or group of people.*

Take a bottle of wine, for example. To a wine expert, it is a Meursault '90, a smooth, dry but mellow wine from a vineyard in Perrières in the Côte de Beaune. If you were prepared to listen, the expert, after describing the wine's taste as 'raspberries and cigar boxes', might tell you about its grape variety, how the vines were grown and what the soil conditions in the area were like. And much more. In the course of the lecture, a lot of technical language – *grape variety* serves as just one example – would be used that would be unfamiliar to those of us who see just a bottle of French white wine.

Most activities and interests have their own specialised language, which is often taken for granted by 'insiders'. They have learnt the language by mixing with people of similar interests or perhaps by reading about it. If you, as an 'outsider', wish to break in, you may find that you first have to acquire a new vocabulary.

In the four columns below, we have mixed up the 'specialised or technical language' that appears in four 'special interest' magazines. Decide what are the subjects or activities concerned and then re-arrange the words so that they are correctly grouped together.

plaintiff	crescendo	base	laptop
concerto	strike	e-mail	cross-examination
tort	logged	statute	innings
database	andante	pitcher	symphony

To give you the experience of being both 'insider' and 'outsider', bring into the next lesson a copy of a magazine connected with one of your own particular interests. If you have not already got a magazine of this type, visit a good newsagent. You will discover the shelves are weighed down with 'specialist interest' magazines; you should be able to find at least one which relates to your own interest, whether it's cooking, travel, fashion, a certain kind of music, films, a sport, motorcycles, photography, or whatever.

Work in pairs, making sure that, as far as possible, each of you knows as little as possible about the 'special interest' of your partner. Swop over the two magazines. You should then look through the magazine you have been given for fifteen minutes or so. List all the words or terminology with which you are unfamiliar. At the end of this time, seek the help of your partner: by the side of each word you have noted, the 'expert' should write a brief definition of the technical term (or jargon).

Finally, pass round the class the lists you have compiled, so that the range of the jargon of various specialised interests may be seen.

Using as a starting point the list your partner compiled in the previous exercise, write a 'Beginner's Guide' to the basic terminology of your own special interest.

Then re-write a section of an article from a specialised magazine, dropping all jargon and using instead words that could be immediately understood by any reader.

- What is the difference in the length of the two accounts?
- Give what you have written to a 'non-expert' to check that you have removed all the specialised vocabulary.

Jargon in everyday use

Just as in the case of particular hobbies or interests, academic subjects such as medicine, the sciences and sociology develop their own jargon in order to provide a kind of shorthand, so that one expert in the subject can communicate easily with another. It often happens that words from a relatively narrow subject gradually become a part of almost everyone's vocabulary. For instance, most people today would probably know what is meant by *class conflict* or *neurotic*.

What specialised subjects do each of the following fairly widely-known words or phrases originally come from? If you have any doubt, consult a dictionary: along with the basic definition of the word, you will usually find an indication of where it originated.

a	recession	**i**	stalemate
b	anorexia	**j**	inferiority complex
c	acid test	**k**	the underclass
d	electoral reform	**l**	special pleading
e	allergy	**m**	catalyst
f	libel	**n**	isobar
g	male chauvinism	**o**	paediatrics
h	genetic engineering	**p**	nuclear fission

Imagine that you have been commissioned by the *Independent* newspaper, which runs a regular column on general topics to do with language, to produce a short article on the way words that were once known only to specialists have entered into everyday use. Draw on the words in the list above and other examples to write the article.

Jargon saves time

Sometimes jargon can be very useful. It saves time to say (or write) of a doctor that she is *an obstetrician* rather than she is *a specialist in the branch of medicine concerned with childbirth and the treatment of women before and after pregnancy*. To demonstrate further the labour-saving uses of jargon, find one expression that will replace all the italicised words in the following five sentences.

1 He recorded the dialogue in the story by using *the actual utterances spoken by the people who were having the conversation.*

2 This computer program is designed to be *easily used by someone who does not know all that much about computers.*

3 The batsman was out *because the ball hit his leg in line with the stumps and would otherwise have bowled him out.*

4 In setting the scene in a novel, pay attention to your choice of *words which identify or describe an attribute of a noun.*

5   We communicate not only by words but by *the movement of our hands and bodies, facial expressions and the mutual bodily orientation of the speakers.*

THE NEGATIVE SIDE

The second definition of jargon in the dictionary reads as follows:

> **jargon 2** *Language characterised by the pompous, often marked by roundabout ways of expression or even gibberish.*

The danger with jargon is that it can be used deliberately to disguise or obscure your meaning, or to make a statement sound significant or impressive when you are really saying nothing of any importance.

Every year, the Plain English Campaign awards a prize to outstanding examples of official language that has been designed to obscure meaning or to confuse people. Here is an example of one winner of this competition – which earned its writer two pounds of best Lancashire tripe. It is the reply to an unhappy traveller on British Rail who had complained about the absence of a buffet service.

> *Whilst I can readily appreciate your frustration at the loss of breakfast, since in the circumstances you describe it is unfortunately true that in many cases where a catering vehicle becomes defective and both stores and equipment need to be transferred into a replacement car, this can only be done during the train's journey. We are very conscious of the need to reduce instances of failure and provide the advertised service to a minimum, and each case is recorded and the reasons closely scrutinised in an effort to avoid a repetition.*

Where are the most glaring examples of the bad use of jargon here? In what ways does the construction of sentences also make the meaning difficult to follow? Re-write this letter, using as simple and clear language as possible.

Clichés and idioms

Jargon may be used by someone who wants to impress his authority on somebody else. A doctor, for instance, is not being helpful when he or she insists on talking about a case of *cardiac arrest* to a patient's relative who clearly does not understand the term; it would be better to refer simply to a *heart attack*.

There is the danger, too, that jargon-obsessed speakers (or writers) simply stitch together ready-made phrases, trying to make themselves sound impressive. What usually happens in these cases is that they produce a string of clichés. A **cliché** is an expression that has started life as a good idea, but so many people have used the expression so often, it ends up dead from exhaustion.

See how many clichés you can squeeze into one sentence; it should not be too difficult, but we will start you off with a few old favourites. We have underlined the clichés for you, just in case there is any problem in identifying them!

1   In this day and age, every avenue has been explored and no stone has been left unturned.

2   The manager was over the moon, but he insisted the team would take each game as it came.

An **idiom** is the kind of everyday, 'ready-made' expression that usually cannot be explained by mere logic: often a comparison is involved. For instance, if you were learning Russian you might come across the expression 'to buy a cat in a bag'. You work out that this cannot mean that someone has actually bought a real cat in a bag. But what does it mean? In fact, a native Russian speaker (or a good Russian dictionary) would tell you that this idiom means to buy something without knowing anything about its quality – and hence something that may be worthless. Perhaps our English idiom 'to buy a pig in a poke' comes fairly close to its meaning.

What do you think would be the equivalent idiom in English to the following six expressions translated straight from the Russian? We give you a short definition of each one in brackets.

1   To talk to someone's teeth (to talk or charm one's way out of trouble)
2   To lay down a pig (to play a nasty trick on someone)
3   To wash bones (to gossip spitefully, to find fault with someone)
4   Not to blow into one's moustache (not to care at all)
5   To bite one's elbows (to be very upset and regretful over some lost opportunity)
6   To sit down in someone else's sleigh (to do something for which one is not suited)

A list of English idioms appears below. You have been asked by someone who is learning English:

a to explain clearly what each expression means;

b whether in your opinion the idiom has been used so often that it is probably best avoided in modern written English.

add insult to injury   to fall on deaf ears   to have a finger in every pie
to hit below the belt   to let the grass grow under one's feet
bury the hatchet   burn the candle at both ends   beat about the bush
keep the ball rolling   pass the point of no return   has an axe to grind
a storm in a tea cup   at the eleventh hour   a fish out of water
have a foot in both camps   a feather in one's cap   a wild-goose chase
a close shave   skeleton in the cupboard   the black sheep of the family
a wet blanket   a hard nut to crack   the thin edge of the wedge

Jargon 'translation'

To demonstrate the deadening effect of the jargon-ridden language which some politicians, civil servants and official persons are inclined to fall into, George Orwell, the author of *Animal Farm* and *1984*, took a beautiful and well-known passage from the Book of Ecclesiastes in the King James Version of the Bible (passage A) and 'translated' it (passage B).

A
I returned and saw under the sun, that the race is not to the swift, nor the battle to the strong, neither yet bread to the wise, nor yet riches to men of understanding, nor yet favour to men of skill; but times and chance happeneth to them all.

B
Objective consideration of contemporary phenomena compels the conclusion that success or failure in competitive activities exhibits no tendency to be commensurate with innate capacity, but that a considerable element of the unpredictable must invariably be taken into account.

- Orwell says of his 'translation': 'This is a parody, but not a very gross one'. What does he mean?
- How much of passage B are you able to understand?
- What qualities does the original passage have that have been lost in passage B?

See if you can do the same as George Orwell did in his example by going to work on this next passage, which is also taken from Ecclesiastes. (And what, you may ask, is the purpose of this exercise? If you do it well, as with the previous exercise on cliché, you should know what sort of writing you should avoid!)

All is vanity. What profit hath a man of all his labour which he taketh under the sun? One generation passeth away, and another generation cometh.

Just to get you started, one version of the first sentence (*All is vanity*) might read: 'At this moment in time, it would evidently appear that every single aspect of our on-going experience offers only numerous instances of the utter and complete impossibility of every achieving any successful and productive outcome.' (The worrying thing about this kind of style is that, once you start, it can begin to come all too easily!)

WORD SQUARES

A word square, not surprisingly, is a square made up of words of equal length that read the same both across and downwards. If the compiler of a word square is very skillful, then the words will read the same not only across and downwards, but diagonally also. Here are some examples of word squares that we have made up, but not, unfortunately ones that go diagonally as well. We'll leave that up to you!

A	S	H
S	H	E
H	E	R

S	E	W
E	V	E
W	E	D

P	L	O	D
L	O	N	E
O	N	C	E
D	E	E	M

D	O	P	E
O	R	A	L
P	A	N	S
E	L	S	E

There are even word squares that contain words of nine letters, but we can't claim to have managed to create any like that! See how many word squares you can make.

Chapter Eight

BAD LANGUAGE

Here are four situations that you may well recognise. Each one would be likely to provoke a strong reaction. For each of these situations, we have provided a number of expressions that people might use in response. Choose the one that you are most likely to use in that situation or, if you think that you wouldn't use any of the ones suggested, write down the one(s) you *would* use.

1   You are late for school. You see a bus at the stop and run as fast as possible to catch it. The driver sees you running, lets you get to the stop and drives away, grinning.

Do you say: **a)** Oh dear!

               b) Never mind. There's another bus in an hour.

               c) Bother!

2   In a vital game from which one point is needed to clinch promotion, your favourite soccer team is trailing 1-0. They are awarded a penalty in the eighty-ninth minute. Their best penalty kicker takes it . . . and shoots wide.

Do you say: **a)** What a pity!

               b) Bad luck!

               c) Ah well, it's only a game.

3   You're going out for the first time with someone you've always liked. You really want to look your best and you've put on your smartest jeans. You accidentally knock over a can of Coke and it goes all over you.

Do you say: **a)** Oh! I've spilled some Coke down my best jeans.

               b) Clumsy me!

               c) Whoops!

4   You've just put the finishing touches to your History project on your word processor and you're really pleased with it. You're pretty sure it'll get an A. You accidentally press the wrong key and wipe the whole project off the computer. It's irretrievable!

Do you say: **a)** Let's start again. My next one'll be even better.

               b) How silly of me!

               c) Gosh!

We doubt very much whether you'd use any of the suggestions we've given you! We'd be very surprised if your language wasn't rather stronger!! Of course, we don't know exactly what you'd say, but we could make quite an accurate guess. The point is that you'd probably use language that is classified as **swearing**. What do all the situations have in common that might lead to the use of swearing?

WHY SWEAR?

In the next activity, we're going to look at some of the reasons why people swear. We deliberately wrote *people* and not *some people* because nearly everybody swears, though there may be a very few exceptions. It's not just you and your friends, not just labourers on a building site nor soldiers in their barracks (to quote two stereotypes) – everybody swears. Your parents, your grandparents, the local vicar, your teacher – even the Queen; they all swear, though they possibly use different swear words than you. What might seem a very ordinary word to you might be someone else's very offensive swear word. And if everyone swears, then the reason for it can't be, as some people have said, because swearers have a very limited vocabulary and can't express themselves properly. University professors of English swear, and no one would say that they have a limited vocabulary!

Here are eight reasons for swearing, together with eight possible situations that illustrate these reasons. Discuss them and match the reason with the situation. For instance, if you think that reason 2 (people swear when they are angry or annoyed) is illustrated by situation d, then you'd fill in a chart as follows:

REASON	SITUATION
2	d

REASONS

1   Some groups of people swear a lot. If you want to show that you belong to the group, then you'll swear as well.

2   People swear when they are annoyed or angry.

3   If you want to abuse or insult someone (or something), then swearing is one way to do it.

4   People swear when they are frustrated.

5   Some people (or groups of people) swear to indicate that they want to be seen as different or separate from others.

6   Swearing can be a way of relieving stress.

7   Swearing can be so much a part of an individual's personality, that it almost becomes a habitual way of speaking.

8   If you swear unexpectedly, it can be a way of emphasising what you want to say.

SITUATIONS

a   Your grandmother has searched high and low for her reading glasses and still can't remember where she's put them.

b   You're just getting ready to go into the exam room to sit GCSE Maths and are chatting to your friends.

c   There's a gang who always hang around in the park after school, and you'd really like to join in as there's a lad you fancy, so you decide to go along with them. You hope they'll accept you.

d   Your dad has been doing some DIY, though he's not very good at it and he's just hit his thumb with a hammer.

e   Your teacher, who is normally very even-tempered, one day surprised the class when she said quietly how 'bloody important' it was to revise thoroughly for exams.

f   Every other word that the man at the gym utters seems to be a swear word, though he never seems to notice.

g   Some Year 9s always travel home together on the same bus and they're always out to annoy all the other passengers by their behaviour and bad language.

h   You really can't stand that girl in your class, as she thinks she's so superior to everyone else, and you decide to tell your best mate what you really think of her.

TABOO OR NOT TABOO?

'Bread off, you cauliflower or I'll smash your eggy face in!'
'Coffee off, burger!'
'You omelette!'

You will probably have realised that this 'conversation' is not taking place between people who are particularly friendly and also that it illustrates one of the reasons we have suggested people swear – to abuse or insult someone. If we'd left gaps like this:

' – off, you – or I'll smash your – face in!'
' – off, – !'
'You – !'

you'd have had no difficulty (though perhaps some embarrassment) in filling in the gaps with suitable terms. In other words, with swear words. You'll have noticed that all the words we have used are to do with food and drink (*bread, coffee, omelette*, etc). We use such words, and all other 'food' words, without any embarrassment in our 'conversation'. But the words we call 'swear words' in English can rarely be used without embarrassment, because they are all connected with subjects that most people normally find difficult to talk about, except with very close friends. There are things we are not supposed to do (like incest or murder) and things we are not supposed to talk about (like sex). These are **taboo** subjects. The majority of our swear words are connected with taboos. The main subjects that form the basis of current British swearing are:

* sex and the parts of the body associated with it;
* religion;
* certain bodily functions that each of us perform daily as we excrete waste matter.

You can see the taboo in operation here in the careful way we have avoided using terms that you must know we know (and use) and that we know you know (and use), but that are often seen as being rude, impolite or obscene. Terms that probably shouldn't be used in a book for schools! No doubt at the end of this lesson as you take a break, these words will be found in frequent use around the school.

Collect as many swear words as you can that are in common use in your group and see how many of them fall into our three taboo categories. You might even use some that mean you have to decide on new categories. Remember not to make any words up, however tempting that might be, as these wouldn't be genuine words in everyday use! You might also find it difficult to decide what does and doesn't count as a swear word.

New tabooos?

If putting food and drink into our bodies were to become a taboo subject for conversation at some time in the future, rather than our bodies getting rid of it, as now, then words like *cauliflower*, *egg* and *burger*, for example, would become the new swear words. In fact, there'd be a far richer and wider stock of words to use!

Below is a list of topics that aren't at the moment taboo, but you never know . . . Choose any of them and write a short piece of dialogue that includes 'swearing', using these new forbidden words. For instance, if you chose cricket, your dialogue might begin: *'Wicket me! What an umpire!'* *she shouted, as her boyfriend told her he'd forgotten the tickets for the concert they were going to see.*

Here is one guideline that you might like to bear in mind when 'inventing' these new swear words; look back at the list of words you collected in your group activity. Collect them together in terms of words beginning with the same syllable or sound. What do you notice? What seem to be the most popular 'opening sounds' for swear words? We sometimes speak of a 'good mouth-filling oath'. Some sounds just seem much more suitable to use when we want to swear. *What a boundary!* is probably much more effective than *What an over!*

cricket	clothes	cars	feet
music	geography	computers	television
your home town	teachers and schools	the weather	flowers

BAD LANGUAGE MAY OFFEND!

We all know that there are situations in which it would be inappropriate to swear. Imagine how you'd feel if you swore loudly in church. Or, when being spoken to by your head teacher. Neither would you be very wise if you swore when being interviewed for a Saturday job! You'll certainly be able to think of lots more examples of when it would be better not to utter those words we all know. It didn't do John McEnroe any good to swear very forcefully at tennis umpires and officials – he was frequently banned from tournaments and heavily fined! Prince Charles seems to be able to get away with it though, as in 1989 he complained that English is 'taught so *bloody badly*.'

However, language does provide lots of solutions: it's possible to swear without people realising that they're actually doing it. We'll look at two of these solutions: **rhyming slang** and **euphemisms**.

Rhyming slang

This is usually associated with Cockneys and probably started when criminals wanted to prevent other people from knowing what they were talking about or planning, but it spread into general use, and today many of us use rhyming slang without realising we're doing so. Let's look at some examples of this 'language in disguise'. You'll quickly be able to see how it works.

apples and pairs = stairs
trouble and strife = wife
mince pies   = eyes
north and south = mouth

Sometimes there's a shortened version that disguises the language even more. For instance:

tit for tat > titfer = hat

Often well-known place names were used:

Hampstead Heath = teeth

Not surprisingly, rhyming slang was often pressed into service to dress swear words in disguise. One of the best known is *Bristol Cities* (*Bristols*, for short) which is used to talk about . . . well, we'll let you guess!

> Here are a number of rhyming slang terms, together with the shortened version if there is one, that are used to disguise swearing. What does your group think the disguised swear words are? Remember what we said earlier about swearing being based on common taboos.

Elephant and Castle	fife and drum
Khyber Pass (Khyber)	raspberry tart (raspberry)
Brahms and Liszt	Barclays Bank (Barclays)
Hampton Wick (wick)	goose and duck (goose)

Can you think of any more? Perhaps your group could make up some new ones!

Euphemisms

You'll remember that a euphemism is a polite or mild way of avoiding saying something we find offensive or taboo. The famous Monty Python sketch in which an irate customer complains about his dead parrot to the pet-shop owner is a good example of using lots of euphemisms to avoid using the word 'dead':

> *This parrot is no more. It has ceased to be. It's expired and gone to meet its maker. This is a late parrot. It's a stiff. Bereft of life, it rests in peace. If you hadn't nailed it to the perch, it would be pushing up the daisies. It's rung down the curtain and joined the choir invisible. This is an ex-parrot.*

There are also lots of euphemisms that can be used instead of swear words. Many of them have been used so frequently that we hardly realise that they are substitutes at all. For example, did you know that *gee, gee-wizz* and *jeepers* are all ways of avoiding saying *Jesus*, or that *darn* avoids having to say *damn*, *heck* avoids having to say *hell* and *gosh* avoids having to say *God*? You'll see from these examples that religious taboos can be very strong!

There are lots more examples of euphemisms for swearing in English. Here's just a short selection. See if your group can work out what the original stronger word(s) might be.

sugar	good gracious	(ee) by gum
blooming	by Jove	Great Scott
shoot	Gordon Bennett	ruddy
golly	crikey	shucks
basket	deuce	naff off
flipping heck	sherbet	armpits
good grief	effing	drat

People often complain that there is too much bad language on television. But exactly how much swearing is there on our screens? Carry out a survey to obtain reliable facts and figures on this controversial topic. To do this, your group will need to watch all the programmes on one evening, say from 7.00 to 12.00, each group member being responsible for watching one channel. Alternatively, your group would watch each evening for a week at the same time, say from 8.00 to 10.00. Whichever method you choose, record the information under these headings:

Name of programme

Channel

Time

Swear words used

Who used them (name/nationality/sex/age)

There's lots you could do with the information once you've obtained it. Think about these questions, for example:

1   Is there any difference between American and and British swearing on TV?
2   In which type of programme is there the most swearing?
3   At what time does most TV swearing occur? Before or after 9.00?
4   Do women swear more on TV than men?

Present your findings as an article for the school magazine or newspaper.

Other fruitful areas in which to investigate swearing are:

- newspapers and magazines (Do the daily papers contain any swear words? If so, which papers use the most? You'll need to look at two or three days' issues to check. Look at magazines aimed at a 'youth' audience (e.g. *Viz*, *NME*, football fanzines). Collect any swear words used. Do they fall into any particular taboo groups?)
- pop music (particularly rap) (Write a short guide or glossary that explains the language used in modern music for the older generation.)

> • school playgrounds (Compile a questionnaire to get children to list the words they would be most likely to use in the playground (a) as a strong insult; (b) when something goes badly wrong; (c) to express great delight or pleasure.

NEXT-DOOR NEIGHBOURS

The following pairs of definitions come from words that are next to each other in the dictionary. For example, 'a light vehicle used by the army' + 'to scoff or make a mock of someone' would lead you to 'jeep' + 'jeer'. Which dictionary next-door neighbours are represented by these pairs of definitions?

1 a person ignorant of religion + a common shrub, usually found on heathland

2 a market or a collection of side shows + an imaginary being

3 a large spiny animal + a sweat gland

4 a hole from which gas escapes from a volcano + to grope about awkwardly

5 a large bird with a huge beak + to come into contact with

6 the fruit of the vine + a symbolic diagram

7 a very soft, white mineral often used for cosmetic purposes + a story

8 healthy and robust + one of two equal parts

9 to govern or to manage + the chief commander of a navy

10 deadly + extreme laziness.

Try to make some next-door neighbours of your own to baffle your friends.

Chapter Nine

LANGUAGE AND GENDER

WHAT'S IN A NAME?

What's your name? How many times have you been asked that question? Where? When? Think of some of the occasions when you might have had to answer it:

- when a new teacher first comes into your class;
- at a party when you're being chatted up;
- when you're applying for a Saturday job.

How many more can you think of?

Do you have a middle name? If you do, do you feel the same way about this name as your first one?

Our names are very important and are often the first thing that people find out about us, even before they've met us. We might have written to them, filled in an application form or they might have seen our names in a class register. People make judgements about us on the basis of our names all the time, though this can be unfair and the judgements may not be very accurate. But names *can* reveal a lot about their owners.

> Let's see what this list of names can tell us. They are all real names of people that we teach at present.
>
> Abida Ahmed, Philip Howard, Helen Walker, Bhupinder Kaur Dhami, Rachael Harding, Vicky Heptinstall, Jaime Tuddenham, Wesley Walker, Sally Robinson, Abraham Cohen, Sabina Uddin, Omer Butt, Jamilah Al-Hargan, James Balderson, Richard Weaver, Romiley Januchowski, Daniel St Quentin, Lai-Han Sung, Maria Rodis, Sinead O'Brien, Mandy Wong, Thomas Ward, Sarah Newton, Liv Haynes, Zackory Lawes, Kane Arnott, Gavern Newsome, Polly Allbones, Adam Davies, Jasbir Singh Gill, Dheemati Perera, Tracy Campbell, Laverne Newsome, Cheung Lan-Ying, Vijay Sharma, Pauline Njuguna, Garfield Simpson, Simon Isaacs.

What can we learn from these names? Remember that the only thing you know about these people is that we teach them and that therefore they are the same age as you.

Working in pairs, see what you can discover from this list. Try to sort them into groups. Which names tell us:

a   what sex the person is;

b   what religious background the person comes from;

c   the country they (or their parents/grandparents) may have come from?

Of course, some names will occur in two or three groups, because it's very possible that a name can tell us more than one thing about its owner. Sometimes, a name can suggest the age of a person as well. Probably not many of you will be called Ethel or Herbert, for instance but it's possible your grandparents or great-grandparents might have been.

When you have sorted the names into groups, as far as you can, discuss these questions:

1   What clues were there to help you put the names into the groups?

2   Did you find first or second names more useful in your discussions?

3   How many countries seemed to you to be represented by these names from one English school? What conclusions can you draw from this?

4   Were there any names that didn't indicate whether the owner was male or female?

Conduct a similar survey of the names of pupils in your own school. Make this survey as large or small as you like, but remember that if it's too small, your results might not be very reliable. Don't survey anything smaller than your own class, but you could look at a year group or, if you are really ambitious, the whole school! Lay out your survey sheets like this:

FIRST NAME	MIDDLE NAME(S)	FAMILY OR SURNAME	COMMENT

Under COMMENT you should include information about such matters as the country of origin, religion or ethnic background and anything you may discover about the history or background of the name. There are all sorts of things your survey could tell you, in addition to the questions we asked about the names we gave you. Here are a couple – but you'll be able to think of lots more:

- How many surnames originally referred to jobs or occupations (Taylor, Clark, Smith, Mason, for example)?
- How many names refer to places or features of the landscape (Bolton, Field, Bridge, Hill, for example)?

When your group has finished its survey, write an article for the school newspaper or magazine about your findings.

MALE AND FEMALE

You'll have found, of course, that a person's first name usually gives information about the sex of its owner, though this isn't true in the case of Sikhs, as their traditional personal names, like Karamjit and Jaswinder, can be used by both males and females. Even some English personal names can be used for either sex: did you know that Evelyn was one of these?

How many names can you find that can be used for either sex? Some names will be spelt differently, but still sound the same, such as *Francis* and *Frances*. (Such words are called **homophones**). Here are some examples to get you started.

SAME SPELLING	SAME SOUND/DIFFERENT SPELLING
Evelyn	Robin (m)/Robyn (f)
Vivian	Leslie (m)/Lesley (f)
Jan	
Lee	

You might find help for your search in books of babies' names written for new parents.

Did you realise that many girls' names are based on boys' names? Think about Paul ➡ Pauline / Paula / Paulette. Or Antony ➡ Antonia / Antoinette. Lots of girls' names are formed in this way – by adding an ending to the boys' name. These endings are usually *-ine, -a, -ette, -ie, -elle, -ina*. See how many names in each group you can find. You already have collected a lot of names in your class or school survey that you may be able to use. Other words, not just names, are formed in the same way. For example:

cigar ➡ cigarette = a little cigar
laundry ➡ laundrette = a little laundry
pipe ➡ pipette = a little pipe
kitchen ➡ kitchenette = a little kitchen
div + ine = div ine = god-like
fel + ine = fel ine = cat-like
mascul + ine = mascul ine = male-like

Any others? Does this mean, then, that Pauline = Paul-like and that Antoinette = a little Antony? Why do so many girls' names come from boys' names? Is it fair that this is the case? Does it tell us anything about the status of girls?

I AM MY FATHER'S SON

Have you ever heard of anyone called Claire Ruthsdaughter? Or William Johnsdaughter? Almost certainly not. But there may well be someone in your school called Claire Johnson or Michael Neilson because there are many surnames like this in English which mean 'son of x'. In these two examples, Claire is 'son of John' and Michael is 'son of Neil'. No doubt, you'll be able to think of lots more similar examples. Your own name may even mean 'son of x'. But why aren't there any surnames that mean 'daughter of x'? In Iceland, there *are* surnames that mean this. For instance, Vigdis Jakobsdottir means 'Vigdis, daughter of Jakob'. There are two other ways in which surnames in Britain can show a male bias:

1   names like *Stevens, Roberts, Peters* and *Andrews* but rarely, if ever, *Margarets, Susans, Christines* or *Alisons*;

2 **Mc** (or **Mac**) in *McDonald*, **O'** in *O'Neill* and **(A)p** in *Pritchard*. These mean 'son of *Donald*, *Neill* and *Richard*' in Scots, Irish and Welsh respectively.

How many other names that follow these patterns can you think of? Should new surnames be introduced to correct the present bias towards men?

TILL DEATH US DO PART

I didn't think I would change my name when I married, but when I looked at the practical side, it seemed too complicated to keep it. (Alison, 30)

I couldn't face getting married if I had to change my name – it's a ludicrous thing to do. (Gabby, 35)

In a 1992 survey of British women, 89% of those who were married had changed their surnames. Only 67% of single women said they were prepared to change. What conclusion(s) can you draw from these statistics?

Carry out your own survey to discover whether people think women should change their surnames when they get married. Your results might be different from the 1992 ones! In order to get accurate answers you'll need to:

a make sure your questions are clear and can't be misunderstood. Not *What do you think about women changing their name when they get married?* but: *Women often change their name when they get married. Do you think that they should?*

(a) *change their name*   ☐

(b) *keep their own name*   ☐

Tick one box.

b make sure you ask an equal number of males and females and that you keep a check of their ages and also whether they are married or not.

There might be other questions that you want to ask in your survey, not just this one. Here are four others for you to think about.

1   Should it be men that change their names when they marry?

2   Should women use *Ms* rather than *Miss* or *Mrs*? *Mr* doesn't indicate whether he is married or not.

3   Until quite recently, boys could be referred to as *Master* (as in Master James Bates, for example), though after a certain age, this term was dropped and young men (even though they remained unmarried) were referred to as *Mr*. Is this term *Master* still in use to refer to boys? If so, in what circumstances? At what age do you think it would be inappropriate to refer to a boy or youth as *Master*?

4   Should husband and wife join their names together, so that if *Miss Smith* marries *Mr Jones*, then their married name becomes *Smith-Jones* (or *Jones-Smith*)?

You'll be able to think of other questions for your survey as well. When you've collected all the information, present your findings as an article in a woman's magazine, as the 1992 survey was.

? TRUE OR FALSE?

True/False 1   Hilary is both a boy's name and a girl's name.

True/False 2   Leone Sextus Denys Oswolf Fraduati Tollemache-Tollemache-de Orellana-Plantagenet-Tollemache-Tollemache was the name of a British officer killed in World War 1.

IT'S A MANS' LIFE!

Does the following paragraph seem odd to you?

'It's a woman's life,' she sighed. 'I've been doing this job for twenty years, woman and girl. I don't know how many woman hours I've put into it, but every girl-jill of you must know how I feel!' Her friends, as one woman, nodded in agreement. 'Yes,' they replied, 'but it's certainly made a woman out of you!'

Try replacing every mention of *woman* or *girl* with *man* or *boy* and see if you think it then sounds more 'normal'. We'll start you off:

'It's a *man's* life,' *he* sighed. 'I've been doing this job for twenty years, *man* and *boy* . . '

Did you have to make any other alterations to change the female references to male? How many people in your group think the changed version is 'normal'? How many thought the first one was 'odd'? Is there any disagreement between the boys and the girls in your group about which version sounded right?

You can tell from this experiment that there are lots of words and expressions in the English language that automatically use a 'male' version rather than a 'female' one. Some people think that this is unfair and shows that the language is biased towards men.

Here are some more examples, this time real ones, that include 'man' words or expressions. For each one, try to find a word or expression to replace the 'man' ones and remove any bias that there might be. We've made suggestions for the first two.

1 Darwin concluded that **men** were descended from apes. (*people, humans?*)

2 He's not **man** enough for the job (*capable, strong, courageous, brave?*)

3 She was wearing a top made from **man-made** fibre.

4 You have performed a valuable service to **mankind**.

5 Kleenex **Man-size** tissues.

6 She wanted to speak to her father **man-to-man**.

7 The telephonists **manned** the phones all night.

8 We've got the **manpower** to do a regular check on all the gates.

Imagine that you are a writing team for a new dictionary called *The A-Z of Non-Sexist Language* and that your group has been told to find acceptable replacements for the following words and expressions. Decide, as a group, what these replacements should be and for each one write a definition for the dictionary and a sentence which will illustrate the new words in use.

right-hand man	manhandle	chessman
he-man	mantrap	man Friday
the man in the street	action-man	a man of the world

HE OR SHE?

Why do you think some people might object to the following sentence?

When a pupil joins a school, he must learn the names of his new teachers.

In the past, *he* and *his* – words which usually refer only to the male – have also been used when both male and female are being referred to, as in the sentence above. This use of *he* and *his* has annoyed feminists, who have argued that there is an in-built bias towards the male in English. In the sentence, there is the assumption that all the new pupils are boys! Only in single-sex schools will this be so. To satisfy these objections, we could write:

When a pupil joins a school, he or she must learn the names of his or her new teachers.

But this seems rather clumsy. Can you see any way of getting round this problem? When one person we teach suggested using *(s)he*, someone objected at once that 'women should not be relegated to being a bracket'!

So far, we have examined language which has a bias against women. But sometimes this bias can work in the opposite direction. How might the following sentences be seen as being biased against men?

Paul Newman

1   The condition of many of our decaying inner cities makes Britain justifiably earn the title: *Dirty Man of Europe*.
2   The vital quality, feminine intuition, often leads us to the right answer.
3   The university authorities were asked to fit thicker curtains in the new hall of residence to eliminate the possibility of Peeping Toms.
4   'Some people might think Paul Newman is over the hill, but those blue eyes still make him my favourite hunk!'
5   All members of the profession must join the Royal Society for Midwifery.

TRUE OR FALSE?

True/False 1	A revised version of the Lord's Prayer begins: *Our Parent who lives in heaven . . .*
True/False 2	The following have been suggested as replacements for *he* to apply to both sexes: *E, hesh, po, tey, jhe, ve, xe, he'er*

JOBS FOR THE BOYS

There are lots of words and groups of words in English that seem to be biased towards men. Think about the names of some jobs, for instance. Many of these words can signal what sex the person doing the job is likely to be. They can do this in a number of ways:

• some words actually include *man* in the name (*policeman, fireman*);

• some words seem automatically to assume that a man will do the job, (*waiter* or *shepherd*, for example), but if a woman were to do it, then **-ess** has to be added to the original male word (*waitress* or *shepherdess*);

• some words seem to imply that, even today, a man will be doing the job, because men have traditionally done so, although women do them as well (*chef, tailor*). The women's equivalents seem to have lower status (*cook, dressmaker*).

A 'dressmaker'

A 'tailor'

Here's a list of jobs or occupations that seem to have sexist names. Invent an appropriate non-sexist word or expression for each one of them.

SEXIST TERM	NON-SEXIST TERM
policeman/policewoman	police officer
anchorman (on TV)	presenter
authoress	writer
stewardess	
dustman	
clergyman	
weathergirl	
spokesman	
dinner lady	
hostess	
ambulance man	
barmaid	
plumber	
housewife	

It is now illegal for employers to say that they want a man or a woman for a particular job when they advertise. They have to be very careful in wording the adverts to avoid sex discrimination and they often have to invent new terms, as you did, like *storeperson* for *storeman*. Sometimes they don't succeed!

Collect as many job advertisements as you can from your local newspaper. Try to sort them into groups like this:

1 jobs that indicate they definitely want a man;
2 jobs that indicate they definitely want a woman;
3 jobs that suggest a man might be more suitable;
4 jobs that suggest a woman might be more suitable;
5 jobs which either sex could do.

Here are a few from our local paper to get you started.

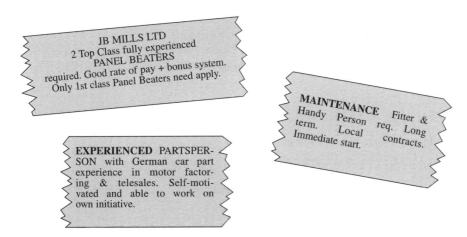

JB MILLS LTD
2 Top Class fully experienced
PANEL BEATERS
required. Good rate of pay + bonus system.
Only 1st class Panel Beaters need apply.

MAINTENANCE Fitter & Handy Person req. Long term. Local contracts. Immediate start.

BARBER REQUIRED m/f, good earnings. Also part time Stylist required. Contact Alan.

EXPERIENCED PARTSPER-SON with German car part experience in motor factor-ing & telesales. Self-moti-vated and able to work on own initiative.

F/T SALES req'd for busy Menswear/Sports shop in M/cr/Salford. Apply in writing ONLY to The Manager.

When you've collected your adverts, here are some questions to investigate:

• How did you decide which group to put the adverts in?

• Were any new job titles invented?

• What methods did advertisers use to suggest they wanted a man or a woman without actually saying so and thus breaking the law?

If you think any of the adverts were sexist in any way, you could write a letter of complaint to the employer, the Equal Opportunities Commission or the Advertising Standards Authority.

TRUE OR FALSE? ❓

True/False 1 The female *daddy-long-legs* is now known as *mummy-long-legs*.

True/False 2 *Herstory* has been suggested as an alternative to *history*.

HOW DO THEY SEE US?

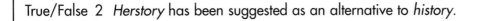

Look at these short extracts from articles which recently appeared in the *News of the World*. They are all describing women:

• pretty, blonde-haired Amber;

• British beauty, Claire Smith;

• mini-skirted stripper, Dee.

The same paper wrote about men like this:

- Robin Lawrence, a former trading standards officer;
- off-licence manager, David Newton;
- Detroit deputy police chief, James Bannon.

You'll notice that the men and women are described in very different ways:

- Amber by her *looks* and *hair colour*;
- Claire Smith by her *nationality* and *looks*;
- Dee by her *clothes* and *job*;
- Robin Lawrence by his *full name* and *job*;
- David Newton by his *full name* and *job*;
- James Bannon by his *full name* and *job*.

Very often, we take these different ways of describing men and women in newspapers for granted and never notice how it affects the way we see the two sexes. But how odd do *these* descriptions seem?

- handsome, red-head Robin Lawrence, a former trading standards officer;
- British hunk, David Newton, an off-licence manager;
- tight-jeaned Detroit deputy police chief, James Bannon.

Men aren't usually described like this in the press!

There are a number of different ways that newspapers have of describing or labelling people: by their age, appearance, hair, clothes, job, gender, nationality, relationships (husband/sister/partner/widow, for example), personal qualities (brave/fun-loving/determined, for example). Each of these can force us to see and think about the people in the way that the writer wishes.

Here are some further examples from newspaper articles. For each one, you should decide in which of the ways mentioned earlier the person is being described.

WOMEN
- Virginia Bottomley, Secretary of State for Health (*The Independent*);
- television presenter, Lisa Aziz (*Daily Telegraph*);
- Miss Grenfell, sister of Peter Grenfell (*Daily Telegraph*);
- superfit Gran, Shirley Leah (*Manchester Evening News*);

- beautiful soprano, Fiona O'Neill (*News of the World*);
- busty, dark-haired Zoe (*News and Echo*);
- the courageous 63-year-old actress, Audrey Hepburn (*Sunday Express*);
- mum of six, Chien Lou (*News of the World*).

MEN

- TV chat show host, Des O'Connor (*News of the World*);
- Douglas Hurd, the Foreign Secretary (*Daily Telegraph*);
- Paul Eddington, star of *Yes Minister* (*The Times*);
- hunky leading man, Omar Ibrahim (*News of the World*);
- fun-loving David Swift, 23 (*News of the World*);
- Bolton Wanderers club president, Nat Lofthouse (*Manchester Evening News*);
- Sir Bob Reid, recently retired chairman of British Rail (*The Independent*).

Copy this chart, marking the appropriate method used.

NAME	PAPER	SEX	AGE	APPEARANCE	HAIR	CLOTHES	JOB	NATIONALITY	RELATIONSHIPS	QUALITY
V. Bottomley	Independent									
Lisa Aziz										

When you have completed your chart, discuss with your partner any conclusions that you can reach about the ways newspapers describe men and women.

You can now take this further and conduct your own investigation into how British newspapers depict men and women.

1 Choose two or three contrasting types of daily or Sunday newspaper: one broadsheet (such as *The Guardian* or *The Observer*); one mid-range (such as the *Sunday Express* or the *Daily Mail*) and one tabloid (such as *The Sun* or the *People*).

2 So that your investigation doesn't become too unmanageable, limit yourself to looking at only one section of the paper (sports news, entertainment pages or news stories, for example). Remember to look at the same section for each newspaper.

3 Make a list of the descriptions of men and women and then complete a chart like the one above.

4 Discuss, in your group, if there are any significant or important conclusions to draw from your research. Then each group should report their findings to the class. Compose a letter to one of the papers you have investigated, explaining what you have found and outlining what changes (if any) you think should be made to its ways of depicting women and men.

PERFECT PARTNERS?

PLUMP 49 yr. old Nurse with sense of humour, who is caring seeks Gent, 40s/50s who is also caring, with own transport.

KIND-HEARTED fun-loving red-haired beauty would love to hear from a loving male for pleasant conversations and more.

PASSIONATE male 30, 6′ 2″, good looks medium build, GSOH WLTM attractive, slimish female 20-33 for lasting relationship.

You'll easily recognise what these three advertisements are: lonely hearts looking for that perfect partner. It's interesting to look at the words the men and the women use to describe themselves in small ads like these. It seems as if there some words that are used only used for males and some only for females. In the following investigation, you're going to see if this is true.

Here are some further examples of lonely-hearts adverts, but this time we've removed any references to male or female. See if you can decide which gender the writer of each of the following is. (GSOH = good sense of humour, WLTM = would like to meet, TLC = tending loving care.)

1 _____ 28, bright, attractive, curvaceous, seeks strong, attractive, sincere _____ 25 – 35 with GSOH for fun/friendship.

2 Skint, deceitful fraudster, 28, tall, dark, handsome, living in dingy flat wants stunning, rich petite, gullible young _____ with sports car.

3 _____ 20s fun-loving with an excellent figure, seeks a muscular, genuine caring _____ for a fun one-to-one.

4 _____ 5ft pretty, petite, bubbly personality seeks TLC from a 30ish, good-looking, well-built _____. You won't be disappointed.

5 _____ Attractive, passionate, athletic, professional _____ 39 with GSOH seeks intelligent, attractive, sensual, adventurous _____ for lots of fun.

6 Hot babe or near equivalent sought by totally undeserving _____.

7 Red-head, sensual, bright beauty, 30s, seeks caring handsome GSOH _____ 35/45 for TLC.

8 Divine _____ sought for love and worship by sensitive, caring 1960 vintage single _____.

Make lists of the words that your group thinks are:

a used to describe women;

b used to describe men;

c used to describe both men and women.

If you want to take this research further, you'll be able to find plenty of examples of your own. They appear in local newspapers and in many magazines. You might like to compose some lonely-hearts adverts of your own that might appear in particular magazines. Here are some (not entirely serious) suggestions.

Farmers' Guardian   *The Beano*   *Just 17*   *Shoot!*

Model Railways   *Vegetarian Life*   *More*   *TV Times*

HIDDEN WORDS

We've hidden one word in each of the following sentences. For example, you can find *herring* in *Give her another ring to see if she'll come out tonight — another ring*.

Which words are hidden in the following sentences?

1 I felt sick as we ate too many chocolates.
2 Get off at her house and then take the second left.
3 I know that no thin girl would ever appeal to me.
4 Will you bring him in directly, please?
5 I'll never go on a roller coaster again because it was the excitement I only wanted, not the fear.
6 Sir Edmund Hillary and Sherpa Tensing were the first on Everest's summit.
7 I'm a lenient person, so I'll let you off this time.
8 He wants your figures to tally with mine.

Now invent some of your own!

Chapter Ten

SPEECH AND WRITING

SPEAK OR WRITE?

Two situations:

1 You're in a shop and see a pair of shoes that you really fancy, but they're not in your size. Do you:

  a write a note to see if there is a pair in your size;

  b ask if there is a pair in your size?

2 You want to go to college after GCSEs to continue your education. Do you:

  a fill in the college application form answering all the questions carefully;

  b phone up and tell the Principal you'll come and have a chat next week?

In each of these situations, the alternative you'd choose is obvious. Writing a note to a shop assistant is both bizarre and not likely to obtain the result you wanted. What these situations do clearly illustrate is that speech and writing can perform different jobs or functions in our society. Sometimes, however, it's not always as easy to decide whether it's better to use one or the other.

Here are twelve everyday situations. Discuss them to see whether you would use speech or writing. You may, of course, think that you need more information to help you reach a decision. For instance, in the first one, you might speak to your mother to apologise for not helping with the washing-up, but feel you must write to the local supermarket manager because you were unable to attend the job interview at the time specified. You should also, therefore, write down what extra information you might need. Or *do* you need to write it down? Remember that there are no right or wrong answers.

1 You have to apologise for something you've done/not done.

2   You need to complain about a faulty cassette recorder you've just bought.

3   You're working in class on an exercise to decide whether you'd use speech or writing in everyday situations.

4   You're applying for a part-time job in a local shop.

5   Someone has asked you to give them instructions on something you're particularly good at.

6   A friend's grandmother has just died, and you want to express your sympathy.

7   You've been asked to describe an accident you've just witnessed.

8   You're planning an essay.

9   You want to persuade people about something you believe strongly in.

10   You need to explain why you're late for school.

11   You've been asked to explain how something works.

12   You're trying to decide whether to leave school or go to college.

Discuss the reasons that influenced your choice of speech or writing. You'll probably need to think about such things as:

- how well you know the person(s) you were addressing (family, friend, acquaintance, colleague, unknown to you);

- the age and sex of the person(s) you were addressing (same age, older than you, younger, same/opposite sex);

- where you are in relation to the person(s) (same room, far away, next to);

- what you were trying to do (complain, persuade, plan, request, express feelings, instruct);

- what type of response you wanted from the person(s) you were addressing.

Are speech and writing different?

Your discussions will have shown you that speech and writing can be used for different purposes and in different situations. But what makes speech different from writing? The list that follows contains a number of different characteristics of language. We want you to discuss them and to put each one under one of the two headings: **Characteristics of Speech** and **Characteristics of Writing**. We've suggested a couple to get you started.

CHARACTERISTICS OF SPEECH	CHARACTERISTICS OF WRITING
Conveyed by sound	Marks on a page
Takes place face-to-face	Participants usually are apart

Usually permanent; Often more formal; Volume, speed, stress are important; Usually impermanent; Usually uses Standard English; Sentences and paragraphs are important; Uses punctuation marks; Has got a lower status; Has got a higher status; Often more informal; Users can get immediate response; Is helped by gestures and body language; Well-organised and planned; Has lots of hesitations and false starts; Has lots of repetition; Usually spontaneous and unplanned.

What does a story sound like?

Here is a **transcript** (a written version of what someone actually said) of the story that a boy, Clive Jones, told in answer to the question: 'What was the most memorable thing that happened to you at primary school?'

er / I remember once when I were at school / I was about six or seven at the time / it were our first biology practical / our teacher / his name were / er / I can't remember his name now / told us he was goin' t'cut up a bull's eye / because we were doin' work about eyes and things / anyway / he went to the small fridge in the corner of the lab / and / pulled out a small dish / and put it on one of the tables in the lab / we all crowded round the table / then he picked up this eye from the dish / ooorrrgh / it were awful / all shiny and bloodshot / then / he / er / put it down on a bit of newspaper / and he / calm as you like / he picked up a scalpel / and cut the eye in two / an' all the stuff in the eye glooped out onto the newspaper / magnifying the text on it / you know / but by this time my stomach was doin' cartwheels / an' I'ad a lump in me throat / so I ran out o' the lab an' straight into the toilet / an' brought up all me cornflakes back into the toilet / if them toilets were any further away / I don't know what I'd've done / an' I got called by me mates fer months after / right[1]

[1] / = a pause

You'll have noticed that this transcript is very different from what Clive would have written in answer to the same question. We've listed for you some of the features of the story that show it's a spoken version. When you've read through them, look back at the story and see if you can add any more examples of these features.

1 *Pauses and hesitations*
   his name were / er / I can't remember his name now

2 *Involvement of the audience*
   an' I got called by me mates fer weeks after / right

3 *Vagueness*
   because we were doin' work about eyes and things

4 *Repetitions*
   and put it on one of the tables in the lab / we all crowded round the table

5 *Exaggerations*
   an' I got called by me mates fer months after

6 *Abbreviations*
   I don't know what I'd've done

7 *Non-standard language*
   the stuff in the eye glooped out;
   if them toilets

Later, Clive was asked to produce a written version of the story he had told. Here's what he wrote. Read it through carefully.

Bull's Eye

I was almost seven when we had our first biology practical lesson. Mr Swinton, the teacher, had been telling us how eyes worked and he decided that it was time for us to see our first dissection. He opened the fridge that stood in the corner of the laboratory and took out a dish. On it was lying a disgusting, bloodshot bull's eye. Mr. Swinton carefully picked it up and put the eye on a newspaper in the centre of a table. We all crowded round. He took a scalpel and began to slice the eye into two pieces. Immediately, liquid seeped from it and ran all over the newspaper, magnifying the text. I felt ill. My stomach began turning cartwheels, and I knew I was going to be sick. I rushed out of the room and dashed for the toilet. I only just arrived in time as all that morning's breakfast of cornflakes and toast quickly reappeared. I'd scored a direct hit on the toilet bowl. My friends never stopped making fun of me for weeks afterwards. 'Bull's eye' they called me!

Here are six statements about the two versions of the story. Discuss each one and decide whether (a) the statement is true, (b) the statement is false, or (c) it is impossible to tell.

1 Both passages contain the same information.
2 The order in which the events are presented is different in the two passages.
3 The written version uses more formal words and structures.
4 There is more repetition of information in the written version.
5 The spoken version seems to have a more planned ending.
6 The written version is more precise.

Conversation play

Whenever you watch TV programmes like *EastEnders* or *Coronation Street*, you are being deliberately deceived. You know that the beer they are drinking in the Queen Vic or The Rover's Return is probably coloured water and that the bar is more likely to be made out of painted plywood than mahogany, but the bar and the beer *seem* real, and that's all that matters. We happily go along with the illusion.

Is the same true of what the characters say? Are the conversations they have just like the ones you'd overhear in a pub any night of the week? Or have the scriptwriters, just like the set designers, created an illusion, in this case, of real speech? You could ask the same question about the conversations found in plays written for the theatre and the radio, as well as TV soaps.

To see if there are any differences between scripted drama and real life conversation, look at these two passages. One is an extract from a play and the other is part of a real everyday conversation. See if you can decide which is which. You'll find it easier if you and your partner read the extracts aloud. After having read the two pieces, fill in the True/False chart which follows.

A

SHEILA   *This is the best one. In three weeks' time, they're coming to start taking them to the post office for the pension and all that. And that's the best. The bloody queue in the post office.*

BRENDA   *When they get there . . .*

SHEILA   Alice Naylor said bugger off to the people in the queue. That'd be the best one . . . she'd be calling police, dead loud. She calls it . .

BRENDA   And then carrying on with the money.

SHEILA   Fancy being in the queue with her. If you know her, you'd laugh, but if you don't . . .

BRENDA   Can she sign?

SHEILA   She signs, but she carries it everywhere, but she signs. But that Norah Daley has no idea even what a pension book looks like, but they'll teach her. But the money, by God with the money, Norah . . . Brenda, Norah isn't that bad with her money actually.

BRENDA   So who is it going to Oldham?

SHEILA   Norah Daley.

BRENDA   Norah Daley.

SHEILA   And Nelly Smethurst. They're going the same. One is gone already.

BRENDA   Is it Nelly Smethurst, the one with the scarf?

SHEILA   Yeah.

BRENDA   Oh, she's nice.

SHEILA   Yeah, she's nice but she's . . . you know, you have to know her really well to know how to work her out . . .

BRENDA   Mmm . . .

SHEILA   Really well. When I'm telling her off, she says John is still working in the insurance.

B

BEVERLEY   Actually, Ang, it's going to be really nice, because I've invited Sue from Number 9.

ANGELA   Oh, lovely.

BEVERLEY   Yeah, so I thought it'd be nice for you to meet her as well. Yeah, 'cos her daughter's having a party. Well, she's only a teenager, so, I said, well pop down and spend the evening with us.

ANGELA   That'd be really nice, 'cos I want to meet all the neighbours.

BEVERLEY   Yeah, just say hello, Ang, and break the ice.

ANGELA   'Cos that was what was so nice when you came over, 'cos it really made me feel at home.

BEVERLEY Well, Ang, I know what I felt like when I moved in – I was lonely. So I thought, well, that's not going to happen to you.

ANGELA   You're the friendly type, aren't you?

BEVERLEY Yeah. Yeah. It's funny, 'cos soon as we met, I knew we were gonna get on.

ANGELA   Well, we're alike, aren't we?

BEVERLEY Yeah. Yeah.

Abigail's Party by Mike Leigh

1   The speakers in A complete what they are saying more often than in B.

2   No one interrupts the other speaker in either A or B.

3   The conversation in B seems more planned and organised.

4   Gossip would be a good word to describe the conversation in A.

5   The speakers in both A and B listen carefully to each other.

6   The speakers in B talk about more subjects than those in A.

7   The speakers in both A and B use casual language.

8   The speakers in A never make any mistakes in how they use language.

	TRUE	**FALSE**
Question 1		
Question 2		
Question 3		
Question 4		
Question 5		
Question 6		
Question 7		
Question 8		

Now, can you decide which extract is the real conversation?

Try writing the dialogue for a short scene from a play. Remember that such a 'conversation' will need a shape or structure. You might find it easier if you improvise the scene with a partner before you begin writing. When you have completed your dialogue, read it aloud, in pairs, to see if it sounds realistic. Here are some suggestions for scenes.

1   A mother and her teenage daughter are arguing about the clothes the daughter is planning to wear to a friend's party.

2   One boy is trying to borrow money from another to pay for his bus fare.

3   Two teachers are discussing the problems they have with a difficult class.

4   Two friends are discussing which film they should go to see at the cinema.

5   A customer is trying to convince a shopkeeper that she/he had been shortchanged.

You can, of course, invent your own scenes.

Speech in writing

When you were writing your dialogues, you might have found it quite difficult to convey exactly how it should have sounded. Authors often have to grapple with this problem of 'putting sounds' into words. Just how do you convey such things as loudness, emphasis, tone of voice, accent and many of the other differences between speech and writing? Here are some of the solutions:

Use capital letters.
'Will you please BE QUIET!' the teacher exclaimed.

Use italics.
'How dare to speak to *me* in that tone of voice?'

Repeat letters.
'Good moooooorning,' he moaned.

Alter the spelling.
As soon as she fund wor it wer, she sheawted, 'Yer greight gawmless foo!' (extract from a Lancashire dialect story)

Use punctuation.
'Don't touch that!!!' she screamed.

Use descriptive words and expressions.
He addressed the class with a hint of menacing violence in his voice.

She whispered softly into his ear.

There are lots of verbs in English that indicate just how speech is uttered. For instance, we've just used some in our examples: *exclaimed, moaned, sheawted (shouted), screamed* and *whispered*. How many more can you think of?

CHORTLE! WHAT A LOAD OF RUBBISH!

GNASHEE!

Comic relief

Some sounds are almost impossible to represent in writing. How can you represent a laugh in written form? Or a cry of pain? A dog growling? A custard pie hitting someone in the face? But writers of the speech bubbles and the text in comics do this all the time! Look at these 'words' all taken from one episode of *Dennis the Menace and Gnasher*:

gnashoo groo chomp huh twang ha-ha pssst har-har aaatishoo plop ho-ho yum gnesh gneesh hmm gneh grrr yum oink

Obviously all the **gn-** 'words' are Gnasher's. But what sounds are represented by the other 'words'? And what do they all mean?

Or look at this selection from *Desperate Dan*:

oh-oh crump ooh oof yip-yip ho-ho ooyah aargh bah ta-da ouch eek

AARGH!

PLOOP!

YUP! THAT'S DAN, ALL RIGHT.

Collect as many comics as you can. Each member of the group should work with one comic and:

a   list all the real words used to represent sounds (like *chomp, twang, plop* and *crump* in the examples above);

b   list all the invented 'words' used to represent sounds (like *aargh, eek, psst* and *huh* in the examples above).

When you have listed all the words from the comics, discuss these questions:

1   Which are the most frequently used invented 'words'?
2   What 'meanings' do these 'words' have?
3   Do the sounds of the 'words' have anything in common?
4   Are the same 'words' found in all of the comics?
5   Is there any difference in the 'words' used in comics written for different audiences? (e.g. young children, adults, British or American readers)

Then compile your own (illustrated?) *Dictionary of Comic Book*

English and write the definitions for some of the words you have collected. Here are two examples:

aargh The noise made when a person receives a sudden and painful blow to the stomach, e.g. when an Indian has been hit by Desperate Dan.

ook The noise made a by a person who has been shocked, frightened or surprised, e.g. someone who sees Gnasher rapidly approaching.

WORDS WITHOUT END

In the following puzzles, you have to find the single word that can be added to the letters provided, making a word each time. For example, if you add *one* to **l-, c-, al-, d-, ph-**, you will get *lone, cone, alone, done, phone*. We've given you a clue to the meaning of the missing word in the first four puzzles and also told you, in each case, the number of letters in the word you are searching for.

1	ch-, l-, w-, cr-, pr-	3 letters	little devil
2	wh-, p-, s-, b-, st-	3 letters	beer
3	t-, pl-, dis-, c-, gr-	4 letters	comfort
4	h-, d-, l-, fl-, dev-	3 letters	yours and mine
5	fr-, tr-, gr-, b-, j-	3 letters	
6	p-, pr-, t-, b-, br-, r-	4 letters	
7	e-, di-, col-, p-, inf-	4 letters	
8	pre-, as-, dis-, re-, ab-	4 letters	
9	f-, gro-, mo-, m-, spo-	3 letters	
10	zit-, rat-, fat-, wit-, bot-	3 letters	

Finally, quite a difficult one! The word you are looking for has four letters.

c-, cl-, dr-, gl-, h-, ho-, l-, m-, r-, pl-

Chapter Eleven

LANGUAGE ACQUISITION

1   Can you read these?

2   What's the French for 'Sorry I'm late, but I couldn't find my bag and I'd put my bus pass in it last night'?

3   What's the Urdu for 'Oh, come on! We're not waiting any longer for them. We'll miss the start'?

4   What does 'Avyernotgorrernutherovem' mean?

5   What does 'Widoantyewkumbaktoeawrowseforrerbitweet' mean?

6   Can you understand this: PECTOPAH'?

Some people who are using this book may be able to answer one or two of these questions, but we bet that there's no one who can answer all six! Northerners will have an advantage with 4 and 5, native speakers of French, Urdu and Russian should cope with 2, 3 and 6 and if you are in the process of learning these languages, you might make a reasonable attempt at those questions. Those of you who can read Arabic, Chinese and Hebrew should have no trouble with 1. Of course, we assume that everyone who is using this book will be able to read English!

These questions will illustrate how difficult it is to learn a language, and if you are struggling to learn a new language like French, German or

Spanish, you'll probably agree. You have to learn new words, new sounds and new grammar, and you've got to be able to read, speak, write and listen to the language (and understand it) if you're to say you've mastered it! It's not easy, is it? Of course, some of you may well be bi-lingual, but even you lucky ones will still find it quite hard to learn a new language. But that's what we've done, apparently without any effort and without realising we've done it! Amazing, but true!

Babies do it all the time! French babies learn French, English babies learn English and Japanese babies learn Japanese, with the result that, by the age of five, children can speak and hold conversations and are on the road to reading and writing their native language. This is a staggering achievement. In this section, we'll be looking at some of the stages on this road.

WHAT DO YOU MEAN?

Here are some things that children nearing their second birthday have said. It's not easy to decide exactly what the children meant, so we've suggested three possibilities in each case. Discuss them in groups and decide, if you can, which is the most likely meaning. Your group may come to the conclusion that more than one of the meanings, if not all, are possible. What further information would you need to be absolutely sure?

Look water

1 *Mummy juice* **a)** I want some more juice, Mummy.
                      b) Put Mummy in the liquidiser.
                      c) Mummy is drinking her juice.

2 *Look water* **a)** I have peed on the floor. Aren't I clever?
                      b) That's a lake.
                      c) Go and find my drink, Daddy.

3 *Daddy kick* **a)** Daddy is trying to play football.
                      b) I'd like to cripple Daddy.
                      c) Let's all cause Daddy intense pain.

4 *See Jack* **a)** Jack is coming up the path.
                      b) I can see Jack hiding behind the chair.
                      c) Let's go and visit Jack.

5 *Only bissies* **a)** I refuse to eat that revolting custard glop.
   (biscuits) **b)** My diet is boring. Can't you think of more
                          appetising food?
                      c) Don't worry. They can be swept up.

You probably found it impossible in your discussion to be absolutely certain what the child meant because you didn't have enough information about:

* who the child was talking to;
* who else was there;
* where the conversation was taking place.

This information is known as the **context**. You can see, then, that the meaning of anything said depends not only on the words spoken, but also on the context in which they were spoken.

Here are some other examples of children's speech. Can you suggest likely contexts and meanings for them?

there teddy   *car want*   *see truck*   *baby here*   *write paper*   *lady draw*

All these examples of children's speech are two words long and, not surprisingly, this stage of a child's language development is known as the **two-word stage**. This two-word stage is just one of the stages in a child's learning of the grammar of English. Obviously, much has taken place before this – children are not born speaking two words at once!

IT'S A MISTAKE!

Most people make mistakes when they learn something new, whether it's falling off a bike or playing the wrong notes on the piano. Learning to use your native language is no different: children do make errors in their speech, and sometimes adults find these errors rather endearing. In almost every case, they disappear in time, but, strangely enough, many of them indicate that the children are learning the language correctly ! Look at this error that Diana, a three-year-old, made in conversation:

There's two mouses over there.

How does this indicate that Diana was learning correct English? Let's look at the stages she went through to arrive at *mouses*.

1   Diana knows the rule for making plurals in English: you must add **s** to certain words (nouns). If there's more than one **x** you must talk about **x + s**. She'll have heard people talk about *cars, pencils, books,* for example. Probably, she'll have heard *houses*.

2   She wants to talk about the two animals she's seen. *One mouse + one mouse = two mouses*, just as *one house + one house = two houses* and *one pencil + one pencil = two pencils*.

3   If all English plurals were formed by adding **s**, Diana would be right – but unfortunately, they're not. Some words don't follow the general rule for plurals. *Mouse* is one of them. (So are *louse*, *child* and *sheep*, for instance. Can you think of any more irregular plurals?) So Diana makes her mistake. But it's a mistake that shows she's well on the way to learning English. In time, she'll learn that *one mouse + one mouse = two mice*.

This type of error is called an **overgeneralisation**. Here are some more examples. Discuss them and show why children make these mistakes by identifying the error, identifying the rule which the child has followed subconsciously and indicating what the correct version should be.

1   I love cut-upped egg.

2   He's more faster.

3   I hurt my foots.

4   It's been leaved there.

5   Why did you kissed her?

Of course, there's more to learning language than just following grammatical rules. Children also have to learn the meaning of the words they hear around them every day. This isn't an easy task. We'd expect you to be puzzled by words such as *resipiscence* and *fletton* and, in the unlikely event of coming across them, you could always look them up in a dictionary, where you'd find that the first means *a change to a better frame of mind* and the second is a *type of brick*. But a child coming across a new word can't go and read the nearest dictionary! It's not surprising that there are a few hesitant steps on the way to learning new words. We'll look at just one of these steps.

When Sophie, a two-year-old, wants to talk about marbles, a ball, a wheel, an orange, radishes and her grandfather's pipe, she uses *ball* whereas we'd use a different word for each thing. Why does she use only the one word, *ball*?

1   She's noticed that all these objects have one thing in common. They're all round. Even her grandfather's pipe has a round bowl!

2   She knows that the round toy she plays with is called a *ball*.

3   She therefore assumes that anything that is round must be a *ball*. She hasn't yet learnt that there are separate names for each of these things.

This aspect of children's language development is called **overextension**. Here are some further examples for you to discuss. Can you see why the child overextends the word? To do this, you'll need to decide what feature the incorrectly named things have in common. We've done the first two for you.

WORD	FIRST USED FOR	LATER USED FOR	COMMON FEATURE
daddy	her father	milkman, postman	male
horse	horse	goat, sheep, cow	four-legged farm animal
hat	hat	scarf, ribbon, hairbrush	
apple	apple	orange, pear, lemon	
tiktok	clock	dripping water	
juice	orange juice	water, Ribena	
milk	milk	the sea, bathwater, fish	
chocolate	chocolate	sugar, cakes, grapes	
fly	fly	breadcrumbs, toes	

For this quite difficult piece of research, you'll need to be able to work with a two- to-three-year-old child who knows you very well. Brothers or sisters, relatives, children of friends would be ideal. We want you to record a short conversation that the child has with you or with someone else and then write it down. Don't be too ambitious – five minutes would be more than enough! When you've written out what the child said, look closely at it to see if you can find examples of the three things you've been working on: two-word utterances, overgeneralisations and overextensions. Can you explain what the child means and why he or she has used them?

LEARNING TO READ

Most of us have no difficulty in reading: we take it for granted, because we do it so often: newspaper headlines, adverts on the side of buses, backs of cereal packets and school books on language – we are constantly bombarded with print.

Talking, of course, comes first: nobody learns to read before learning to talk, and it doesn't come as naturally to us as speech. You have probably forgotten what learning to read was like, but in this activity, we'll try to remind you. You'll need to work in pairs.

Words that are printed backwards will be quite difficult for you to read easily, especially as you aren't used to reading such 'mirror' printing. A similar situation faces young children as they begin to read on their own: printed words are difficult to follow, and they may not know what the text is about.

Sam was a person of very few words, so when he said it was all brilliant, we knew he meant it. And that was strange because, of all of us, Sam was the one who least wanted to go.

It was just before Whitsun last summer and our class was herded into a coach one drizzly Monday morning. Along with Miss Dewar and a couple of other teachers, we were off to spend a week on a farm in Devon. The school went there every year, and this year it was our turn.

One of you should read this 'mirror' text aloud. The other person should listen very carefully to the reading and note down any hesitations and errors that their partner makes. When you've 'read' the text aloud, discuss what you noticed about the reading. These questions should help you in your discussion.

1   Where did most of the hesitations or errors occur? At individual words? At punctuation marks? At the ends of lines?
2   What would have made the text easier to read (apart from the obvious!)?
3   What made the reading sound unnatural?
4   Did you understand what you were reading? How did you try to make the reading easier for yourself?

This activity should have given you an idea of why learning to read – with understanding – is quite a challenge for young children!

Books for kids

Of course, children learn to read best when what they read is interesting and enjoyable – story books are one of the most enjoyable ways of all. There are lots of exciting and beautifully illustrated books written for young children today; you probably remember reading them yourself and may even have kept some of them, just as you may have kept a favourite cuddly toy.

Here are three short extracts from story books that are (or have been) used to help children in an infants' school learn to read. In each of them, a dialogue is taking place. Read them and decide in your group if they are likely to achieve their aim. In your discussion, remember that children learn to read most successfully when what they read interests them and when the language used in their books is similar to what they themselves use and hear. How close have the authors come to writing language that children will have come across in their daily lives?

1

Once there were three baby owls:
Sarah and Percy and Bill.
They lived in a hole
in the trunk of a tree
with their Owl Mother.

The hole had twigs and
leaves and owl feathers in it.
It was their house.
One night they woke up and
their Owl Mother was GONE.
'Where's Mummy?' asked Sarah.
'Oh my goodness!' said Percy.
'I want my Mummy!' said Bill.
The baby owls thought
(all owls think a lot) –
'I think she's gone hunting', said Sarah.
'To get us our food!' said Percy.
'I want my Mummy!' said Bill.

Owl Babies by Martin Waddell

2

(Burglar Bill has stolen a baby by mistake).

Burglar Bill bounces the baby on his knee.

'So you can talk,' he says. 'Say Burglar Bill.'

'Boglboll,' says the baby.

'Say Peter Piper picked a peck of pickled pepper,' says Burglar Bill.

'Boglboll,' says the baby.

Suddenly Burglar Bill feels his knee getting wet and smells a smell.

'Poo,' he says. 'I know what YOU want!'

'Poo,' says the baby.

Burglar Bill changes the baby's nappy. He doesn't have another one, so he uses an old bath towel instead.

'Say For he's a jolly good fellow for changing my nappy,' says Burglar Bill.

Burglar Bill by J. & A. Ahlberg

3

(Peter and Jane are at the seaside.)

Jane and Peter play in the water.

They like to play on the boat.

'Come on,' says Peter.

'Come on the boat.'

'Come and play on the boat.'

'Jump up. Jump up here.'

Jane is in the water and Peter is in the boat.

They want to fish.

'Get in the boat,' says Peter.

'Get in the boat, Jane.'

Things We Like by W. Murray

Try writing your own story for young children (aged five to seven). Before you start, it would be a good idea to do some research. You ought to spend some time reading books that have been written for this age group to see what established writers have done. Think about:

- how long your story should be;
- its shape: there should be a strong and easily followed plot;
- what subjects will interest your audience;
- the language you will use. Look carefully at the vocabulary, the grammar and repeated patterns in the language;
- whether you want to illustrate it.

Remember that the language children meet in these early stages of learning to read should be close to what they already speak and hear. If you can illustrate the story, so much the better. To get you started, here are a few suggested opening lines:

> Down in the valley, there were three farms. The owners of these farms had done well. They were rich men. They were also nasty men. All three of them were about as nasty and mean as any men you could meet. Their names were . . .

Fantastic Mr Fox by Roald Dahl

> One evening, a little girl named Dinah Price kissed her mum and dad goodnight, climbed the stairs – and found three bears in her bed.

Ten in a Bed by Allan Ahlberg

> Something very strange was happening to Treehorn. The first thing he noticed was that he couldn't reach the shelf in his closet that he had always been able to reach before, the one where he hid his candy bars and bubble gum.

The Shrinking of Treehorn by Florence Heide

> Plop was a baby Barn Owl, and he lived with his Mummy and Daddy at the top of a very tall tree in a field. Plop was fat and fluffy. He had a beautiful, heart-shaped ruff. He had enormous, round eyes. He had very knackety knees. In fact, he was exactly the same as every baby Barn Owl that has ever been – except for the one thing. Plop was afraid of the dark.

The Owl who was Afraid of the Dark by Jill Tomlinson

You might like to take your finished story into a local school to get some genuine customer feedback!

LEARNING TO WRITE

Learning to read and learning to write are almost like two sides of a coin: you rarely find one without the other. We've already looked at the challenges that children face when they learn to read; now we'll see how they cope with early stages of writing. As with the reading activity, we'll put you in a similar situation to that faced by young primary school children. The 'mirror' passage that you worked on before continues:

> Sam had his granddad there to see him off, a tall, white-haired man who always carried a silver-topped stick in one hand – from his army days, Sam said. Everyone knew Sam's granddad; he collected him from school every day. But I knew both of them better than anyone because they lived in the flat next door to us on the same corridor.

Sam's Duck by Michael Morpugo

Copy out this passage, but use the hand you don't normally use. You won't find this easy! Have a look at what you wrote and then compare it with your normal writing. List any differences between the two (e.g. letter size, shape . . .). Did you find it more tiring than your normal writing? Why? Did your 'wrong hand' writing look as you wanted it to? If it didn't, you probably will have felt annoyed or frustrated!

You're likely to realise now how difficult learning to write can be. But young children face added difficulties! You would have had no problems in understanding the passage you copied out, but this won't always be the case. Nor will they always know how to spell difficult words. The next activity should give you an insight into the extra difficulties they face.

Rodin

One of you should choose a short passage (from an encyclopaedia or reference book, say) on a subject that the other person knows little or nothing about. It's best if the passage contains unfamiliar words or names. Read it aloud to your partner and then ask him or her to write a summary of what they've heard – again using the 'wrong' hand. You can read the passage more than once, but don't answer any questions about spellings. Here's an example of the sort of passage we mean.

Rodin was born in Paris on November 12, 1840, the son of a police official. He studied art in a free school for artisans and on his own at the Louvre, because he was refused admittance to the École des Beaux Arts. For many years, he worked for other sculptors, including Ernest Carrier-Belleuse. Rodin collaborated in the early 1870s with a Belgian artist on architectural sculpture for the Bourse in Brussels.

Encarta 95

After you have finished, compare the original with the summary. How accurate was it, considering the subject matter was unknown? What methods did you use to cope with the spelling of unfamiliar words? Were there any other problems?

Let's look at what very young children *do* produce when first they start to write. Each of these pieces was written when Clare, Kate and Hanif were four and a half and had been in nursery class for a short while.

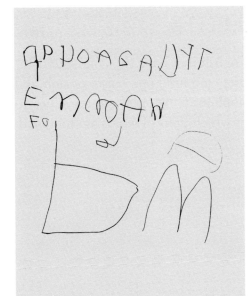

What have the children learnt about writing? What can they do? Here are some points to consider in your discussion:

- Size of letters?
- Which letters are recognisable?
- Position of the writing on the page?
- Capitals or lower case?
- Shape of letters?
- Are any words recognisable?

Clearly, Clare, Kate and Hanif have already achieved a great deal in their short writing careers!

SOUND BITES

There are a large number of words in English that have the same sound but different meanings. As an example, there are *night* and *knight* or *stair* and *stare*. Such words are known as **homophones**. Below there are clues to more homophones. See if you can spot which pairs of words are involved.

 1 seven days; feeble
 2 created; a female servant
 3 a young male; a floating warning
 4 a plan; windy indoors
 5 an equine animal; with a sore throat
 6 part of a window; it hurts
 7 seven make a week; rather bewildered
 8 delivered by the postman; masculine
 9 naked; Yogi
10 build up; demolish
11 driven by the wind; where bargains are found
12 bells ringing; part of a lemon
13 metal; shown the way
14 a bundle of cotton; cricket equipment
15 enlarged; a deep moan
16 conceited; indicates wind direction
17 looks at; take forcibly
18 used to propel boat; source of metal
19 not good; ordered
20 the eldest child; it's all around you

Chapter Twelve

LANGUAGE IN SCHOOL

STORIES BY KIDS

We've given you the chance to write a story for young children and to look at examples of their very early writing. Now we're going to look at some of the stories that children themselves produce in school.

All children love stories. They love having stories read to them either at school or at home; you probably remember your teacher reading a story to the class or your mum or dad reading to you at bedtime. And, of course, children love writing their own stories and hearing them read aloud or displayed on the wall of the classroom. Again, you may remember doing this yourself at primary school and may have even kept some of what you wrote at that time. One of the most popular writers for children is Roald Dahl, and he wrote a story called *George's Marvellous Medicine*. George makes a medicine for his repulsive grandmother – she suggests to George that earwigs are the best part of the lettuce – into which he puts ingredients he finds in every room of the house. The results for his grandmother are rather surprising: smoke comes out of her mouth, she hovers in the air and then starts to grow so tall that her head comes out through the roof!

After listening to *George's Marvellous Medicine*, one class of six-year-olds was given the chance to write its own *Marvellous Medicine* stories. They were asked what they would put in their medicine, who they would give it to and what they thought would happen. They were allowed to do 'free writing'; the teacher just wanted the children to write and set their imaginations racing. Here are four of the stories they produced.

One day my mum sed I am
going to go to the shop's. So
you willl have to take your cunsung's
medsen. So Laura did. But
Laura's cunsnng was so horddide
to Laura that she didn't wehnt
to take the wret medsen.
So Laura got a big kun
and got same theggs to put
in the medsen. She put toof best
in it and sope in it and
bullous bath in it and then
she went in the bed room.
she look on har mums
dressing teddily She fond
leppseke and puffume and that he
was all. Then she went to the
kuincne and she fond snggr and
spor and thet is all.
Then she went in and guvu
her medsen to har cunsung
so she went in and cunsuna
spining har cunsuna wnet
and then a rond and around.
wook then he did all the

LAURA
cunsung = cousin   kuincne = kitchen

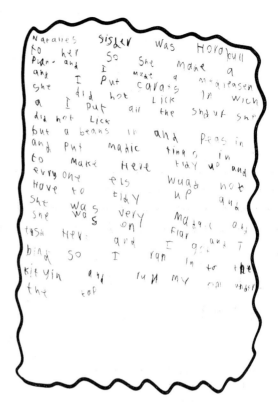

Nataties sister was Horobull
to her Plan. and I So she make a
any I make a m-aieasen
she did hot LICK in wich
a I put all the shduf sh
did hot LICK
but a beans in and peas in
and put mafic tinng in
to make Heve tidy up and
evry one els wugg not
Have to tidy up and
she was very Magig ang
she was on flar and I
tysa Heve and I get and I
bind so I ran in to the
kit yin and tuu my
the tap

NATALIE
shduf = stuff   tasd = touched   bind = burned

One day Louis was haveing a barbe-
cue But Louis thorght there
wasent much Food Betwenall
of them so he seid to himself I cald try and make
something that vould make
them grow Bige. So he wint in
the hase and Looked he Fook
some/asalenea and some BROWN haiy srfg
ant some toothpaste and some
creme and some water. He cook ed it
and stered it he thorght it ned
more so he put a bit of Perfume in
handsome coffe the cooked it agen
an sdered it agen. then he went
out side and pored it on the Food
he pored it on the ribs and I sn nice
made them Biger so he pored it on the
Fool then thay all had a

LOUIS
ending is: so he pored it on the food and thay all had a party

one day I went to a park and I saw a
flower. I picked it and took it home.
And planted it in my garden. When
I saw dads most biggest plant. I wanted
to make mine even more bigger than his.
And I wanted to let myne grow
even more buttiful than his. So I
decided to make a medicine I put
in a little bottle of perfume.
And a little bag of growing powder.
And a tube of toompast. And
then I boiled in an oven then I
tested it on another plant.
It worked the plant lost its polem
and started to grow. And then Sude-
nly a smell that was so nice. So
he new it would work then
it was for real. He put it on
its polem the polem fell off
and started to grow polem.
something had gone rong it
grew on the first plant So
why did this one not grow.
I no the polem fell off and
dident grow back. Well you
can't win all of them

NICKY

138

Imagine that you were the teacher of the class that had produced these stories and the children had asked for your opinion of what they had written. What would you say to them? Remember that the greatest encouragement teachers can give children is when they respond more to the *content* of what was written than if they keep pointing out any mistakes the children might have made! You'll know this from your own experience – it's better if your teacher praises the good things you have done, rather than forever picking out errors you make in grammar, spelling and punctuation.

As you decide what you want to say, think about what the children already know about writing stories. Do they, for instance, know that the best stories:

- have a shape (a beginning, a middle and an end);
- usually follow a chronological sequence of events;
- will be convincing because they are based on what the writer knows about the world around him or her;
- will interest the intended audience (in this case, the children themselves)?

What would you say if parents complained that their children were not being taught about handwriting, spelling and punctuation?

1

Stories are not the only type of writing that children do. In any infant or primary school, they'll be writing, for example, diaries, lists, reports, instructions, greetings cards – and many other types as well. Collect, either individually or as part of a group, as many examples of young children's writing as you can. Then devise a script for a short radio programme called *Young Writers*, in which children's work is read out together with a brief linking commentary that showed why you'd chosen the pieces.

2

You, or your parents, may well have kept examples of your writing from your earliest days. If so, you have a very good resource for research. Look at how your writing has changed over past years. Consider such things as:

- spelling, punctuation and grammar;
- the content of what you wrote;
- whether your handwriting has changed;
- the various types of writing you are now an expert in.

SECRET LANGUAGE

So far, we've been looking at children's 'official' language: the language they use in school stories and other writing and when they talk to grown-ups. But as you'll probably remember, there's a whole range of what we might call 'undercover' language that children use between themselves, language that most adults have forgotten about (though they will certainly have used it when they were children) and that children keep strictly to themselves. No grown-ups allowed! We're talking about such things as nicknames, riddles and jokes, insults and the words and expressions they use to organise business between each other – swapping, keeping promises and so on.

A few years ago, a collection of children's unofficial language was published, which had been gathered from primary and secondary schools all over the country. Here are just a few examples of what children were saying and laughing at some forty years ago. The strange thing is that almost the same expressions were found as far afield as Scotland and Cornwall and that many of them dated back hundreds of years. Children must have access to a secret Internet! Or is there another reason?

Nicknames

Kids then, as now, had nicknames for almost everything and everyone. Here, for example, is what two schoolboys wrote down when asked to give the nicknames of their classmates:

Phumph, lumber bonce, lush, Gables, square head, pugh, Jimpy, Hepsiba, lofty, big head, Rudolth, hog, scoffer, flippin kid, rocker box, chubby cheeks, clink, cocoa, Cowson, Screawy, nuts, bolts, tweedle, gilly, ruby nose, Bullet Head, nutty.

Parts of the body

These, too, are given nicknames. Here's a selection of the more printable ones:

head: *nut, loaf, bonce, block, dome*

nose: *conk, beak, snitch, snout, snot-box, bokio*

hands: *mitts, dukes, paws*

Approval words

You'll have lots of different terms for expressing approval. In the chapter on slang, we asked you to list some such terms you currently use and we pointed out how quickly these kind of words go in and out of fashion. You'll probably find that these examples from the 1950s are very different from the ones you use today:

super,   smashing,   beezer,   bonza,   lush,   smack on,
spiffing,   spiving,   whizzing,   swell,   whizzo

Clever people

There's always someone really clever in your class, isn't there? He or she has probably been called *genius*, *brains*, *professor*, *brilliant bonce*, *jingler*, *clever dick*. You may even recognise the *swot*, *swotpot*, *plodderoner* and *bookworm*. Then there's the *nosey-parkers*, the *snobs*, the *cribbers*, the *swankpots*, the *starecats*, the *scaredy-babies*, the *cry-babies*, the *creeps* and *crawlers* . . .

Jokes, riddles etc

Kids love jokes, riddles and the puzzling questions known as conundrums. Here's just a few collected in the 1950s. You'll no doubt have come across ones very similar.

What's the difference between a prison warder and a jeweller?
One watches cells and the other sells watches.

Why did the window box?
Because it saw the garden fence.

What key is hardest to turn?
A donkey.

What did the window say when the tree fell through it?
Tremendous.

What does a diamond become when placed in water?
Wet.

Knock, knock.   *Who's there?*
Arthur.   *Arthur who?*
Arthur Mometer.

And so on, and so on.

Parodies

Children also like making up mock versions of well-known songs and even hymns. Have you heard these alternative carols?

While shepherds washed their socks by night
All seated round the tub
A bar of Fairy soap came down
And they began to scrub.

We three Kings of Orient are
One in a taxi, one in a car,
One on a scooter blowing his hooter
Following yonder star.

1

You saw what a wide range of nicknames just two boys produced. What are the most 'popular' nicknames in your school? To discover the answer, each member of your group should be responsible for collecting the nicknames from one form or class in each year. You'll probably need to ask only one member of the class to supply you with this information. Make sure you record the real name of the person who is being referred to! Here are some questions to ask when you've collected the information.

- Are nicknames used much in your school?
- Are girls given nicknames less frequently than boys?
- Are there any differences in the way each year group uses nicknames?
- Do they die out as children move up the school?
- Are nicknames based on surnames, first names, personal characteristics or . . . ?
- Are the nicknames friendly, jokey, rude, hurtful? Or none of these?

You could carry out a similar survey on the nicknames you have for your teachers!

2

Your group should collect as many jokes, riddles and conundrums that younger children tell and find funny. You'll no doubt remember some that made you laugh (or groan!) when you were younger, but there's lots of other people you could collect from: teachers, parents, grandparents, relatives and, of course, younger children themselves. You may be surprised how many people can remember once you give them a few hints or prompts. Once you've got a sufficient number, write and publish your own *Bumper Fun Book for Kids*. You'll be continuing a tradition that stretches back hundreds of years.

3

Produce a dictionary of children's 'secret' language that this time lets adults in on the secret! Here are a few examples to get you started.

bags   A word used to indicate that a child claims immediate ownership of something as in *Bags I this one.*

barley   A word used to obtain relief or mercy when playing a game; or when a child wants to drop out of the game.

fains   An alternative word for *barley* used in the south of England.

SCHOOL REPORTS

You might not like them. You might wish they didn't exist. You might not want your parents to read them; but we'd be very surprised if *you* didn't read every word of them with the greatest care. 'What did he mean by that?' 'She can't say that. It's not fair!' 'That's rubbish! I *have* tried my best.' 'It's his fault. He can't teach properly.' 'Great! I've always liked Miss X.'

Reports are one of the highlights of the school year and, though you might not believe it, many of you will probably keep your reports well into adult life. Ask your parents or relatives if they've kept theirs. Many of them certainly will have. Of course, in the old days, you didn't get a chance to reply to the comments made about you, but now some schools encourage you to do just this on report forms that can build up into your Record of Achievement.

Here are extracts from four school reports. Two were written recently and two are from the 1950s. You'll see how they've changed over the years. The first two are from primary and the second two are from secondary schools, including one from a school that allows its pupils to write their own comments on the work they've completed. Look at them carefully to see how teachers (and pupils) are using language. What differences do you notice in the reports? Compare them with the reports that your school produces.

CHURCH ROAD C.P. JUNIOR SCHOOL
REPORT

Term Ending: *July 1955.*   Class: *3A.*

Name: *Susan Jones*   Position: *1/47.*

SUBJECT		REMARKS
English	*92%*	*Two highly creditable results.*
Arithmetic	*98%*	
Social Studies	*V.G.*	
Art and Craft	*G.*	
Other Subjects & Activities	*V.G.*	*Shows deep interest in stamp collecting.*

GENERAL REMARKS

A keen, conscientious worker, who has made splendid progress.

Signed: *A.M. Stott* Class Teach.

Very creditable results & well deserved.

Signed: *A. Lump* Headmaster.

Parent's Signature: *H. Jones*

TECHNOLOGY
Lucy has designed and constructed models to accompany work achieved in other curriculum areas.
She has developed an ability to communicate and evaluate these technological activities.

HISTORY
Lucy has communicated her understanding of historical facts using old photographs and Victorian artefacts.
She has shown an ability to describe and explain historical change relevant to her personal history.

GEOGRAPHY
Lucy has demonstrated that she can follow directions and observe and talk about a familiar place.
She has expressed her increasing knowledge and understanding of her local environment.

OTHER SUBJECTS
Lucy has developed a greater awareness of the different religions and cultures in our community.
She has continued to appreciate all forms of music, drama and P.E.

FURTHER COMMENTS
Lucy has shown leadership qualities through her willingness to assist her peers.
She has also developed a greater initiative and independence whilst working on her own or with others.
She has also proved to be reliable and responsible.

ATTENDANCE: Actual: 310   Possible: 340   Times Late: 1

Class Teacher *J. Mutton*   Headteacher *Michelgate*

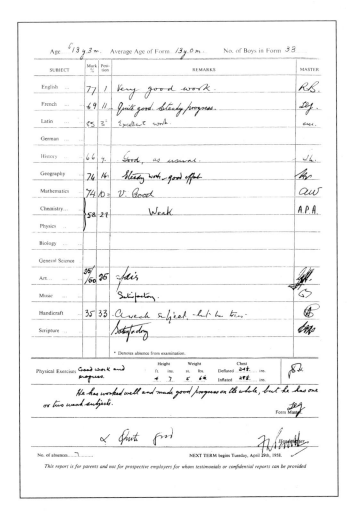

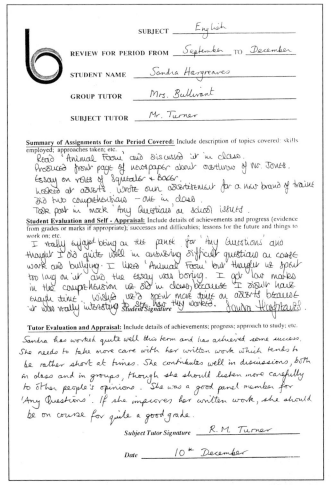

You've seen the way school reports have been written; now it's time for you to turn the tables and write some reports of your own. Here are three topics for you to choose, together with some suggested headings. Remember, you could be treading on some dangerous ground here!

- **Teachers**: knowledge of subject / teaching methods / interest of lessons / topics covered / quality of marking / class control / attendance / punctuality.

- **Schools**: quality of staff / facilities – libraries, labs, specialist rooms, etc / food / quality of buildings / interior decoration / sports and societies / examination results.

- **Parents**: fairness / generosity / discipline / quality of meals . . .

There are lots of other topics you could choose, of course: a local shop, a club, lollipop ladies . . . etc.

SCHOOL RULES

All organisations have rules and regulations; schools are no exception. Rules are usually written in a very formal and sometimes off-putting language. They seem to be saying to everyone who has to read them: 'We are very important and we want to make very sure that you know this. Therefore we will speak to you in very important sounding language. Pay attention!' Here's an example of the regulations from one high school.

Meadowbank High School Regulations

The following regulations have been drawn up in the interest of all members of the school.

Meadowbank High School expects every pupil to act responsibly at all times and to this end you are required:

1 To treat all members of the school, including other pupils, teachers and support staff, with courtesy and consideration at all times.

2 To respect school property and the property of members of the school community.

3 To help and not obstruct the educational opportunities of other pupils.

4 To comply with all subject requirements.

5 To attend all timetabled classes.

6 To complete all assignments and homeworks according to the standards and deadlines set by teachers.

7 To participate fully in class activities.

8 To dress in the standard school uniform.

9 To refrain from smoking.

10 To eat and drink only in those areas designated for this purpose.

A pupil who commits any act of gross misconduct may be suspended at once by the Headteacher who shall report this misconduct to the Chair of Governors.

Gross misconduct includes but is not restricted to:

* assault or harassment or physical violence of any kind

* cheating in examinations

* any offences relating to drug, alcohol or solvent abuse

* carrying anything that can be used as an offensive weapon

* theft

Rewrite these rules in a less formal style, but make sure that they still indicate to pupils that they must be obeyed. For instance, instead of:

Meadowbank High School expects every pupil to act responsibly at all times and to this end you are required:

1   To treat all members of the school, including other pupils, teachers and support staff, with courtesy and consideration at all times.

you could write:

Meadowbank High School pupils must always act responsibly and therefore you should:

1   always be polite and courteous to everybody in school.

Now imagine that you are a member of your school's Student Council and that the Headteacher has asked it to draw up a new set of rules for the school. Write the rules that you would like to see the school adopt.

LIPOGRAMS

A novelist called George Perec once wrote a book in which he deliberately avoided using the letter **e**. In the whole book there was not one single **e**. This is really difficult to do, as **e** is the most common letter in the alphabet. We've used thirty-four so far! Here's a short extract from another novel in which Ernest Wright does the same thing:

Upon this basis I am going to show you how a bunch of bright young folks did find a champion . . .

Avoiding using one particular letter when you are writing something is called a **lipogram**. See if you can do the same thing. Don't cheat by using uncommon letters like **q**, **x** and **z**!

Chapter Thirteen

ADVERTISING

Think of the last time you bought something that cost quite a lot of money – perhaps it was a Walkman or expensive trainers. What made you choose a particular make or brand of the item in question? Were you influenced by any of the following factors?

- your feelings about its appearance and performance;
- the price compared with similar brands;
- the fashionable label;
- what your friends had previously bought;
- reports in magazines such as *Which?* about reliability and value-for-money.

Were you aware at all of being influenced by any advertising?

Look in your local paper and you will find the columns of its Classified Adverts section full of this kind of advert.

Jewellery

LADIES ELLESSE Performance watch. Bi-colour bracelet/white dial. Ex. cond. In presentation box. Was £275. Will accept £95 o.n.o. Tel 0008-9-445 8063

This advert for a second-hand watch packs in quite a lot of information.

- What do *Ex. cond* and *o.n.o.* mean?
- Why does the advert state *Was £275. Will accept £95 o.n.o.* and not *This watch originally cost £275. I will accept £95 . . .?*

Now compare this form of advertising with the advert opposite. Presumably any reader of the Classified Advert for the second-hand watch would be looking through the columns in the newspaper with a definite interest in buying a watch. Would this be true of most readers glancing through the *Independent* magazine, from which the second advert is taken, over a late breakfast on a Saturday morning? Probably not. So the first thing that this advert has to do is to grab readers' attention and stop them turning the page.

- How is the reader's interest captured?

- Why have this particular woman and man been chosen to appear in the advert?

- Consider the layout of the advert. For example, where does the information about the product appear? Why is it placed in this position?

- Does the slogan *Designed to Perform* refer solely to the watch?

GET A SLOGAN

In the last advert we have looked at, you will see that a slogan acts as a kind of headline: *Designed to Perform*. The advertiser uses the slogan to strike a keynote in connection with a product. If the slogan sticks in your mind, so much the better. For example, can you fill in the missing word in the following slogan: *Beanz meanz . . . . .*? If you can, the advertiser's sales slogan has lodged the brand name firmly in your memory.

To make a slogan memorable, advertisers use many of the techniques that you might find in a poem. For example:

- rhythm and rhyme: *Gillette – the best a man can get.*

- alliteration (the repetition of a consonant): *Guinness is good for you.*

- puns and plays on words: *Together we make Sun Alliance.*

- personification (speaking of something as though it had human qualities and feelings): *Midland: the listening bank.*

- metaphor and simile (comparison): *Kellogg's Corn Flakes – it's like eating sunshine.*

Advertising slogans often make use of unusual spelling, too, as an attention-grabbing trick. For example: *Drinka pinta milka day.* Which of the other devices noted above does this slogan also use?

List as many advertising slogans as the members of your class can remember in five minutes. Then look closely at each of the slogans in turn and consider:

- which of the techniques we have just outlined are used by the advertisers to make the slogans 'catchy' and memorable;

- whether there are any other effective, attention-grabbing techniques used which we have not mentioned.

IT'S ALL A MATTER OF IMAGE

When you were considering the advert for Ellesse watches, you probably decided that it was significant that the two people pictured in the advert are young, glamorous and attractive. The woman gazes out at us with a kind of 'keep-your-distance' arrogance; she is clearly poised and sophisticated. Her hunky partner does not look in our direction; perhaps he is lost in a world of his own smouldering passion. It is pretty certain that we are meant to understand that this couple are more than just good friends. Look how their bodies are intertwined. What is significant about the positioning of the picture of the man and woman's watches that almost cradles the two figures?

The two people are, of course, pictured in swimming costumes. Why? This is surely not meant simply to show that these watches are waterproof. The situation – and it is obviously not taking place in the local swimming baths – allows the picture to display two attractive young bodies. In addition, the Ellesse watches are linked with a certain life style that is healthy, athletic and sexy. The couple represent a cool, self-assured and exclusive existence. Like the watch, they are designed to perform. The advert is suggesting to us that if we buy an Ellesse watch, we may also be able to break into their world and achieve the glamour and sophistication of this pair.

There is more to say about the advert, but we have at least started to describe the image that the advertiser is trying to create for Ellesse watches. When we speak of an **image** in advertising, we are referring to the qualities and feelings that are linked with a product. Most advertisers work on this principle: 'Discover what the people we are seeking to persuade really want in their lives, and then make them believe our product will give it to them.' You may buy a watch but, perhaps without knowing it, you are also buying an image and a life style.

Many adverts make the kind of appeal which suggests, by various means, buy 'Product X' and you will achieve:

* glamour and good looks;
* attractiveness for the opposite sex;
* a healthy life style;
* luxury, status and wealth;
* self-confidence and popularity;
* successful business careers;
* a contented and secure family life;
* the enjoyment of knowing that you belong to a select few who set fashions and trends.

1 Which of the qualities listed on the previous page are *not* included in the 'image' of Ellesse watches?

2 What kind of product might in an advert portray an old couple, gazing contentedly into a log fire?

As well as appealing to our desires for material wealth and status, adverts may also prey on our fears and anxieties. For example, the advert that appears on the previous page dates back to the time when companies marketing credit cards were trying to persuade consumers that a piece of plastic would give them a great advantage.

1 What does the advert suggest about the life of the man in the foreground who clearly possesses a Barclaycard?

2 What is the significance of the fact that the crowd in the background are portrayed as faceless?

A COLLECTION OF ADVERTS

• Find adverts in newspapers and magazines that show in practice how advertisers link a product with an appeal to those 'desirable qualities' we mentioned in our list – appeals to 'glamour and good looks', 'attractiveness for the opposite sex', and so on.

• Identify cases where the appeal is limited to one or two central ideas. And where whole clusters of different desires and aspirations are suggested by an advert.

• In the light of your study of a range of adverts, does anything need to be added to our check-list of those qualities that advertisers believe influence people?

The best way of finding out about adverts is to look at particular examples and to analyse the effect that the advertiser is trying to achieve. For the project that follows, we shall continue to concentrate on advertising that appears in newspapers and magazines. Each member of the class will need to bring three or four examples of adverts and be prepared to say how the adverts in question seek to persuade us to buy a particular product. If you tear out pages, be sure to make a note of the publication(s) in which the advert(s) appeared.

> We would like you to concentrate on four areas, three of which we have already discussed.
>
> 1 What gives the advert its eye-catching quality?
> 2 Is the slogan a good one? Why (not)?

3 By what means does the advertiser create an 'image' for the product?

The fourth issue you should consider is:

4 What kind of language is used in the advert?

In this area, here are a few things to look out for.

- Language which makes a direct appeal, often in the imperative (that is, as if giving an order): *Buy one today!*

- Language which makes great claims, often using adjectives in the superlative (that is, a claim that X is the best or most desirable product): *X washes whitest and gets rid of even the toughest stains!*

- Language which, while claiming a lot, is nevertheless difficult to pin down. For example, *More people are watching Sky News.* (Does this mean that more people are watching Sky News than did so a few months before? Or are more people watching the News on Sky than on the BBC or ITV?) Other examples of this kind of intentional vagueness are: *X is proven to be better* (proven by whom?) or *Y costs less than you think* (how much do you think?)

- Language which builds to a climax. For example: *It's newer, It's crisper, It's lighter, It's the new Ryvita!*

- Language which uses compound expressions (that is, joins several words together) such as *day-in-day-out freshness* or *up-to-the-minute design* or even invents new words: *Pampers nappies are designed to hug-move.*

- Language which uses wit and humour. For instance, in a campaign for Heineken lager, the advertiser first established the slogan *Heineken refreshes the parts that other beers cannot reach* with tongue-in-cheek references to a range of activities and problems that the lager was claimed greatly to improve. Then, in the second stage of the campaign, the word *parts* in the slogan, which of course contains a *double-entendre* (that is a play on words that has a sexual double meaning), went through several variations; in a number of adverts, *parts* was jokingly replaced by words (accompanied by the matching pictures) such as *partings* and even *pirates*.

These are just a few preliminary guidelines. You should be able to add points of your own about the general use of language in

> advertising. For instance, compile a list of the words you find used most frequently in advertisements. Then arrange the words into groups which show what the words have in common. (One grouping might be: *free, bonus, bargain, save, extra.* What is the common feature that these words share?)

Follow up your study of magazine and newspaper advertising by looking at adverts on television. The best way of doing this is to record an evening's adverts on a video cassette which can later be played back to the whole class. As well as the points you considered in your analysis of advertising on the page, be aware of the way the film is edited and cuts from one image to the next, and the effect of music and a 'voice-over'.

THE AGENCY

The advertising campaigns we see on television, in magazines and on hoardings are put together by special organisations called advertising agencies, which employ people with expertise in such areas as market research, psychology and art and graphic design. When a new contract is offered to an advertising agency, one of the first questions that the team assigned to the campaign will ask is: 'What are the strengths of the product concerned – and what are its weaknesses?' In the second category, the main problem will often be that there are many competitors. How is the product, therefore, to be given an image that will make it stand apart and achieve a special attraction in the eyes of the public? Sometimes the problem may be more specific. A direct approach to it may be the best one. Polo has been advertised for years as *the mint with the hole*, although if you stop to think about it for a moment, the hole in the middle means that you get less mint. Cadbury's Flake chocolate is very fragile; it is liable to break up and get all over your clothes. Yet the advertising of the product insists *Only the crumbliest, flakiest chocolate tastes like chocolate never tasted before.*

Look at the advert for a continental lager beer that appears below and decide:

- What do you think is the major problem in selling this product that the advertising agency has identified?

- How is this 'problem' dealt with in the advert?

- What section of the market does the advert aim to reach?

The last question we asked you to consider about the Löwenbräu advert guides us to a second vital area. At the first stage of any advertising campaign, the team from an agency will ask: 'At which section of the public should the advertising be targeted?' The advertisers will need to find out who is buying the product already. The young or the old? One social class more than another? Men more than women? And is it going to be possible to extend the existing market in some way? Deciding on the potential audience – the target – for the advertising will affect both where adverts are placed – the *Sun* as well as *The Times*? – and the approach and tone adopted in them.

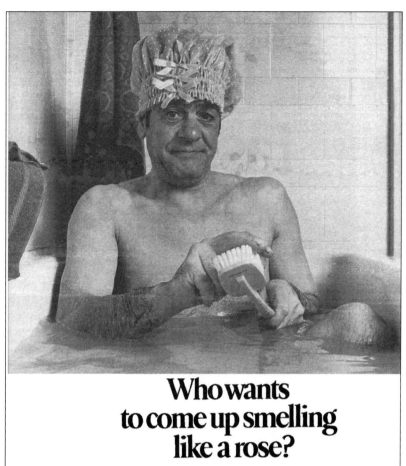

Look closely at the advert for Wright's Coal Tar Soap. Bearing in mind the readers that would be targeted in each case, which of the magazines listed below do you think the advert appeared in? And what are the clues in the advert, both in the picture and its words, that indicate the intended audience?

- *The Soap Mag*: a trade journal for people in the soap industry
- *In the Cab*: a magazine designed for long-distance lorry drivers
- *Woman's Own*
- *Radio Times*
- *Sunday Times Magazine*

Follow up this question of the targeting of different audiences by advertisers by working on the following project in groups of four or five. Each group should select two publications which have strongly contrasting readerships. For example:

1   *The Sun / The Times*;

2   *Vogue / Hello*;

3   any 'teenage' magazine of your choice / a publication such as *Warwickshire Life* (they exist for most counties!);

4   *Viz / 'Q' magazine*.

Make a list of all the advertising in the two publications you are looking at, noting in each case the product concerned and the size of the advert. Then work out a rough percentage for the total amount of space taken up by advertising in relation to the rest of the publication. What do the type of product and the 'images' portrayed tell you about the different readerships of the publications concerned? Each group should report its findings to the rest of the class.

CHANGING IMAGES

As the members of a team at an advertising agency, you have been asked to change the image of the following products so that they reach a wider part of the market. Again, work on this project in groups of four or five, each group having chosen one of the products listed. Your job is to prepare a report in general terms in which you decide:

*   how the image of the product must be altered;

*   where you would place adverts in order to reach this wider market.

You should also include:

*   a sales slogan and rough sketches of the adverts you intend to appear in newspapers and magazines;

*   a script for one or two adverts for radio (maximum length fifty seconds) which your group will perform for the rest of the class.

1   Gerontozade has been advertised for many years as the kind of glucose drink you would take if you were recovering from an illness. However, its makers now wish to persuade young people that it is a trendy drink; that not only is it a good idea to drink Gerontozade after exercise, such as sports or working out in the gym, but that its refreshing taste may be enjoyed at any time.

2   Bergolvo is a family saloon car manufactured in Norway. It has a tremendous reputation for safety, economy and reliability, but this has meant that its sales have been almost completely narrowed down to elderly drivers. You have been asked to combine the old image of Bergolvo with an appeal that will attract younger drivers; you need to communicate the idea that a Bergolvo car is quite sporting and fun to drive.

3   Snugfit thermal underwear is very 'practical' in cold weather, but market research has shown that very few people under forty ever wear it. Comments made by both men and women in the age range of fifteen to thirty were very much along the lines of 'I wouldn't been seen dead in those old-fashioned kind of long johns' and 'Even if it was freezing, you'd have to be about to draw your old age pension before you wore Snugfit.' Design an advertising campaign that will change such people's minds and persuade them to give Snugfit a try.

DISCUSSION

Before you embark on the final exercise in this chapter, which is to design a full-scale advertising campaign of your own, consider the following general questions about the nature of advertising.

1   In what areas would you expect advertising to be keenest and most competitive? Why?

2   How do you react to the following comment made by a student who had been working through this material?

'It's all very well to analyse these clever techniques used in advertising, but I'm sure that most people would miss the point and not be affected at all. After all, you do not usually study adverts – you only look at them at most for a few seconds.'

CRUDGEHAM'S ALES

This assignment should be done individually. Compare the finished campaigns and decide which are the most convincing ones.

Crudgeham's Ales, a medium-sized though rapidly expanding Nottingham brewery, has decided to invest heavily in increased brewing capacity and to launch a new lager. As well as selling the lager in its own 205 tied houses (that is, public houses owned by the brewery), the company intends to market the lager to the free trade (off-licences and the 'club market') and to the big chains of supermarkets. The lager will, therefore, be dispensed in 'draught' form in pubs, and it will also be sold in bottles and in cans.

As a key member of the advertising agency (B. F. Fudgit Inc.), you have been asked to write a preliminary report which outlines the campaign you would mount on Crudgeham's behalf. At this stage, there is no limit on your budget, though later you may have to compromise! As this is a new product, you have been asked to give your advice about:

- The choice of a brand name, giving the reasons for your suggestion.
- The design of the can for the lager and of the label for the bottled lager, along with related marketing features, such as the badge or emblem that will appear on dispensers in pubs. (Some rough sketches will be important here. Be specific about your choice of colours.)

In your report you should also cover the following points:

- What is your view of the essential problems in introducing the product to the market? How are these difficulties to be overcome?
- What section of the market will you be aiming at? (For example: the young/old; the affluent/working class; men/women.)
- What kind of 'image' do you intend to give the product? What emotions, needs or feelings are you going to make an appeal to in order to sell this brand of lager? (Of course, this image should be the co-ordinating feature of the whole campaign.)
- What are your ideas for sales slogans?
- In what media will you concentrate your campaign? Can you justify the cost of television advertising? Newspapers? (*The Sun* or *The Times*?) Magazines? Commercial radio? Street hoardings?
- Draft out in sketch form (or describe) some of the adverts you intend to appear in newspapers/magazines.
- If you plan to use television, having justified the expense of this form

of advertising, write a script for the advert(s). (This should be set out in the format of a play.) Do the same for any radio adverts.

Remember, the whole aim of your report is to persuade the directors of Crudgeham's that you have the right ideas and that your agency is capable of mounting the kind of campaign that will really launch the new lager to a successful start. Give a lot of thought to the order in which you present the points you wish to make.

ALL THE SAME

Angela Alsop avoided all aeroplanes and airports avidly. Aiming at arriving at Adelaide, Australia after an ambitious afternoon at an auction, Angela accepted an appropriate and agreeable aperitif afore ambling afoot.

Not the world's most elegant or interesting sentence, as we're sure you'll agree. But can you do any better than us? Have a go at writing a sentence in which all the words begin with the same letter and which makes some sort of sense. It's not easy!

Chapter Fourteen

NEWSPAPERS

If you think about it for just a moment, the idea that newspapers are concerned only with the news is not true. We asked the members of one of our classes what they particularly enjoyed in the newspapers they read. The following items were singled out:

- details about television programmes;
- gossip about film, television and rock stars;
- competitions;
- comic strips;
- astrological forecasts (read surprisingly widely, but never, of course, taken seriously!);
- crossword puzzles.

What other items in newspapers do you like to read? And what items do you never bother to look at? Make a list of your 'likes' and 'dislikes'.

HOLD PAGE TWO!

Work on the following exercise in groups of four or five. Each group will be nominated by the teacher as the editorial team of a particular newspaper – the *Daily Mirror*, the *Daily Express*, the *Guardian* and so on. Twelve potential 'stories' are summarised below. As the deadline draws near, there is room for the inclusion of **three** of these items on an inside page of the newspaper. The editorial team of each newspaper has to make a selection, justifying the choices they have made with reference to what they think is likely to appeal to their readers.

1 The Chancellor of the Exchequer has announced that the bank rate will be reduced by 0.5%.

2 The star of a soap opera has been convicted of drunken driving.

3 A demonstration against the government in Sri Lanka has turned into a riot in which twelve people were killed.

4 A scientist in California has come up with a theory that eating lots of ginger increases a woman's chances of becoming pregnant.

5 The Belgian Prime Minister has announced that there will be a general election in his country in a month's time.

6 A parson in Birmingham has started to hold religious services in a nudist camp.

7 The Queen has had to postpone a visit to open a soap factory in Dorset because she is suffering from influenza.

8 Pierre Corneille, the leading figure of French fashion, has said that in his designs for the summer season the mini-skirt is set to make its return.

9 The Professor of Folk Life Studies at The University of Truro has been given a grant by the local tourist board to write a history of the Cornish pasty.

10 At question time in Parliament, the Prime Minister stated that there were no plans to increase the old-age pension.

11 A woman of seventy-five was severely beaten up in her home in Sunderland by a burglar and robbed of three pounds.

12 There are totally unsubstantiated rumours of a lucrative business deal agreed by the directors of Manchester United Football Club by which, in return for a large sum of money, they have agreed that their sponsor's name must be stamped in indelible ink on the forehead of all spectators as they pass through the turnstiles at the next home match.

Have we got 'news' for you?

How many of the stories listed above would you describe as 'hard news' and how many amount to little more than the trivial? Which of these stories would *you* be interested to read about? Why (not)?

Over the last twenty years or so, many newspapers, particularly those at the popular end of the market, have moved away from a coverage of the daily news in any detail to concentrate on more general items – the 'human interest' story and features and gossip about 'celebrities'. What do you think are the main reasons for this trend? Consider, for instance, the influence of television on the newspaper industry.

READ ALL ABOUT IT!

For your work on the next part of this chapter, you will need to arrange to bring into class on one specified day as many of that day's newspapers as possible. (Include some local newspapers as well as the 'nationals'; it will be interesting to see how the former variety differs from the latter.)

Split up into groups of four or five. Each group should prepare a report for the rest of the class on one particular newspaper. The points we would like you to consider are:

1 What are the distinctive features?

Every newspaper aims to make its appearance distinctive, so that a reader has only to cast an eye over one page to know 'That's the *Sun* – or *The Independent*'. How is this style achieved? Look at such things as:

- the heading of the title page;
- size and layout;
- the way columns are spaced;
- the type of print (Are different kinds and sizes of print used? If so, for what purposes?)
- the length of stories and their number per page;
- the standard length of paragraphs;
- the relation of text to headlines and sub-headings;
- the use of photographs and any graphics, such as sketches or cartoons.

2 What is the general make-up of the newspaper?

What is the balance between stories devoted to 'hard news' and other items? List, in percentage terms, the amount of space given to different subjects. We are not looking for exact mathematical accuracy here – an approximation of this kind will serve our purposes:

- stories connected with home news: 10%
- human interest stories: 25%
- gossip: 15%
- special features: 10%
- foreign news: 5%
- sports: 10%
- advertising: 15%
- women's pages: 5%
- television programmes and preview: 5%

3 What kind of reader is the newspaper aimed at?

Would you say, for instance, that the paper would appeal to one social class more than another? To young or older people? To women more than men? What level of education does the paper assume in its readers? Is there, for instance, any coverage of detailed political commentary, international affairs or developments in the arts and sciences? Or does the paper contain a high proportion of stories and gossip about the popular media – personalities in television, pop music and films? And how difficult is the crossword puzzle?

The kind of readers the newspaper is trying to reach will be reflected in the range of stories and features covered. And also in the kind of language it uses. In general, for example, do you find:

- simple or complex sentences?
- basic or demanding choice of words?
- the use of Standard English or a 'chatty', informal style?

The style and range of the advertising that appears can be revealing about the 'target' audience. Is there, for instance, a lot of adverts for 'prestige' items of furniture and household goods?

Look closely at the news stories and the editorial in the newspaper and decide whether the paper has any definite political point of view of its own. (Does the language used, for instance, to describe the policies and actions of government ministers reveal any strong bias 'for' or 'against'?)

We would expect you to end up with some kind of personal statement about the newspaper your group has been looking at. Did it interest you? All of it, or only parts? Why (not)? Did everyone in the group share the same general opinion? Would *you* buy a copy of the newspaper tomorrow?

VERSIONS OF THE NEWS

As each group reported on its findings about the newspaper it had been studying, you probably found that certain comparisons between newspapers arose naturally. Maybe one paper had a story on its front page which was simply not mentioned at all by another. Of course, what is omitted – as well as what is included – by a newspaper must reveal a great deal about that paper's priorities.

Very often the best way of defining the particular nature of a newspaper is to compare its treatment of a story with the approach adopted by (a) a similar type of paper – for example, the *Mail* compared with the *Express* – or (b) a different kind of paper – for example, *The Sun* contrasted with *The Independent*. The next activity, involving short discussions between the groups that have been studying particular newspapers, is designed to encourage comparisons of this kind.

Select one news item that was covered by all (or nearly all) the newspapers you have been reading. Then bring together, to form a series of combined groups, the teams that have been previously studying two newspapers. So, the members of the class who have been studying, say, the *Daily Mirror* meet with the group that has been looking at *The Times*, and so on. Discussion involves comparing notes on the different treatments of the single story you have decided to concentrate on. Some guidelines for your discussion appear below. After ten minutes, all the groups change round and, after having made as many comparisons as time permits between different papers' approach to the story, you should be ready for a 'whole class' discussion of the contrasts that have emerged. Focus on the following points:

- What degree of importance does the paper give to the story? This will be revealed by its position in the paper, the size of print used in the headline, the length of the article and the kind of language used.

- What was the tone of the article? Was it, for instance, sensational and dramatic or detached and largely factual?

- Were there any factual differences between the stories?

- Did any of the accounts focus on a different aspect of the story?

- Were quotations from people involved introduced into the story? What effect did these have?

- Were you aware of the opinion or feelings of the writer of the article and if so, how was this expressed? Or did the writer remain impersonal?

- What (if any) use was made of photographs?

Every picture tells a story

Arrange for each member of the class to bring a photograph that has been cut out of a recent newspaper. Try to choose photos which, in one way or another, are striking or thought-provoking. The photos, possibly pasted onto sheets of A4 paper to make them more durable, should be distributed round the class. (Make sure you do not receive your own choice of photo!) Then invent and write up the story that you think might have accompanied the photo in the pages of (a) a 'popular' tabloid newspaper, and (b) a 'quality' newspaper.

HEADLINES

Both the content (what is said) and the style (how it is said) of headlines establish much of the 'tone' of a paper. Some headlines 'scream' at you; some are calm and dignified. Headlines are important because most people do not read a newspaper from cover to cover; they scan the pages, looking for what interests them. The headline-writer hopes to invent something that will act like the bait on a fishing hook.

Headlines in the popular press are often designed to produce a lip-smacking, 'you-must-read-this' impact – the kind of sensationalism, for instance, of the GANG KILLER'S LOVE NEST WITH MP'S DRUGGIE WIFE variety. It is the combination of the supposed respectability of being a Member of Parliament's wife with sleaze of *Gang Killer's Love Nest* and *Druggie*, which is intended to grab the reader's attention.

You will probably have noticed that, again particularly in the popular press, headlines are written in a unique kind of language.

100 JOBS AXED AT CAR PLANT

The men at the car factory concerned would never say: 'Our jobs are in danger of being axed'; the director of the company involved would not say to a colleague: 'I am going to axe a few jobs today.' The special language of newspaper headlines has been developed because of the need to dramatise the essence of a story in a short space. Take another headline:

HOLIDAY FOOD BUG HUNT

To object that this statement is not a proper sentence – does it contain a verb? – and that it is not entirely clear would be to miss the point. It is certainly snappier and more eye-catching than FOOD ANALYSTS ATTEMPT TO LOCATE THE SOURCE OF FOOD POISONING IN HOLIDAY RESORT. Words such as *axed* and *bug* (to mean illness or virus) are typical of newspaper headlines – a part of their unique language to which we referred earlier.

Make a glossary – an alphabetical list of words with definitions or explanations – of the kind of language that tends to appear only in newspaper headlines. This is a short example of the kind of glossary we have in mind:

blasts: strongly criticises
bonanza: large amount of money, often a windfall
cuts: reductions
rift: disagreement
plea: public appeal or request
probe: inquiry
quit: resign
quizzed: questioned
scare: alleged problem, crisis
scoops: wins
swoop: co-ordinated arrest or investigation mounted quickly and secretly by a large number of police

Not surprisingly, two words you will probably come upon time and time again in headlines are *drama* and *dramatic*: DRAMATIC BRIDGE DEATH; GAZZA TRANSFER DEADLINE DRAMA, etc. What other words are used very frequently in headlines?

Making the headlines

Look carefully at the headlines in the newspapers you have collected and see if you can find any examples of the following two 'tricks' that are often used by headline-writers.

Plays on words

These are produced by puns or the recycling of well-known phrases. For instance, a story about a vicar who had been caught out doing something stupid might be typically given a headline such as MAN OF THE CLOT. On the same page, we came across a story about the wedding of a famous tennis player (TENNIS ACE WEDS SMASHER) and another (WHAT AILS CROWN?) which turned out to be not about the Royal Family, but a pub that had run out of beer. Such is the itch that many headline writers have for puns, they tend to intrude into even the most serious news items: for example: SUICIDE BOMBER BLASTS PEACE TALKS. Headlines also tend to feature alliteration – the placing of words which begin with the same letter: BRUM BUTCHER'S BONANZA.

Intentional ambiguity

Something which is ambiguous can be understood in at least two different ways. Headline writers have a lot of fun with headlines of the GENERAL FLIES BACK TO FRONT variety. Particularly in the popular press, they are also very fond of *double entendre*. An article, for example, headed WIVES SPURN GOOD REPRODUCTION actually concerned a survey of the purchase of hi-fi sounds units which allegedly showed that housewives tended to be the group least interested in paying a lot of money for stereo equipment. The *Sun's* headline for one cricketing story was WE'VE GOT 'EM BY THE GOOGLIES.

Does the nature of headlines vary much from the so-called 'quality press' (a paper such as *The Independent*) to the tabloid, 'popular' newspapers? Locate one story which has appeared in several newspapers and compare the headlines it has been given.

SCHOOLKIDS' HEADLINE FUN BONANZA!

The next activity is designed to give you some practice in the headline-making skills you have been considering. It is a game which you should play in pairs. The scoring system is entirely optional.

First, select a newspaper you have not seen. One of you reads out a headline; the other has to say what the story that follows will be about. Score a point for anything that comes reasonably close.

For the second round, one of you reads out a story; the other has to invent a headline. See what headline the piece in question was originally given, and score a point if the one you come up with is as good – or better. You may need an umpire to give a final decision in this part of the match!

Write a story – make a headline

Each member of the class should write a short news story on one side of A4 paper in the style of a particular newspaper. The story could concern something in the news at present or an event that has taken place in school recently. Then distribute the news items round the class. Each member of the class should read the story he or she has been given, and then devise an appropriate headline for it. Write the headline on the reverse side of the sheet. At this point, the teacher should collect in all the papers and, reading out the headlines in turn, determine if the original writer of the story is able to identify his or her story by the headline that has been chosen for it.

Making the front page!

Turn back to the list of potential news stories we gave you on pages 161 and 162. Working in groups, select one or two of the stories and produce a replica copy of the front page of any national newspaper which, underneath appropriate headlines, deals with the stories in the style of the newspaper concerned. You might want to adapt pictures cut out from newspapers to paste up on your page. If you have access to a word processor, it should be possible to produce a 'mock-up' that comes very close to the real thing – and one which would make a very effective wall display.

FEATURES

In the rest of this chapter, we are going to look closely at an example of newspaper writing:

The special feature

The feature writer is not sent out to report on 'hard news.' A feature is a more leisurely kind of writing in which the journalist inquires into a particular topic – or individual. This might involve interviewing someone in the public eye and producing a 'what really makes X tick' account. Or perhaps the editor of the newspaper wishes to give readers some insight into the current state of the coal-mining industry, and so a reporter is sent out to research the subject: preparation for the article that is to be written will probably involve a visit to several coal mines and interviews with a range of people who work in them or have control over them.

The background to the following feature by David Selbourne was a widely reported speech given by Prince Charles in 1991 on the subject of English teaching in schools. In this speech, Prince Charles was critical of 'falling standards' in spoken and written English; he also claimed that schoolchildren were no longer obliged to study the great authors of our

national literature, such as Shakespeare, and that, as a result, we were in danger of producing 'an entire generation of culturally disinherited young people'. So, no doubt with his reporter's notebook in hand, David Selbourne went out to look at the situation as he found it in several comprehensive schools. The article he wrote for *The Sunday Times* (1991) appears on the next page. Read through it now.

We wish to focus principally on the particular slant that David Selbourne gives to this feature (question 6), but to get you talking about the article first, we would like you to first discuss questions 1 – 5.

1 Summarise what Tim Small thinks is most important about education.

2 What do you think is the purpose of the method Peter Malin used to introduce Chaucer to a class? How successful do you think it would be?

3 On several occasions, there are references to a 'traditionalist' view of education. What do you learn from the article about this view?

4 What is Jo Reid's attitude to reading?

5 What kind of 'evidence' does David Selbourne draw on in this article?

No writing is without bias. Even when we attempt to be objective – to see things unclouded by our own personal opinions and background – it is always going to be the case that something of our outlook will be evident in what we write. Sometimes a judgement may be **explicit** – directly stated – and sometimes it may be **implicit** – hinted at or implied. In question 6, we want you to consider how objective David Selbourne is in the feature article and to what extent his own views are communicated, both explicitly and implicitly.

6 (a) To start you off, we would like you to consider the following extracts. What do they reveal about David Selbourne's attitudes towards what he sees in particular and to what he thinks in general about education?

> . . . *it (the revolution in education) is all over bar the shouting, and is irreversible in its essentials. (column 1)*

> *(Minor outbreak of tittering, and no wonder.) (column 1)*

> *'What if a kid wanted to do a project on the Beano?' I asked Jo Reid . . . (column 2)*

Today's lesson: Shakespeare is not needed

David Selbourne finds out what teachers and pupils think about our 'cultural heritage'

Sit in almost any comprehensive school classroom and, if you didn't know it already, you'll see and hear that a revolution has taken place in education. Moreover, it is all over bar the shouting, and is irreversible in its essentials.

Prince Charles (Gordonstoun and Cambridge) may be 'sad' that we are in danger of producing an 'entire generation of culturally disinherited young people' who have never read Shakespeare, 40% of our children may leave school without qualifications, and parents may tremble. But Tim Small, director of studies at Peers comprehensive school near Cowley – the most disadvantaged catchment area in Oxfordshire – still thinks the purpose of the educator is to 'match children's needs'. 'I do not define a successful education in terms of which facts people know,' he said to me with swift-speaking confidence. 'There are no absolutes in terms of a body of knowledge.'

So if reading Shakespeare doesn't 'match a child's needs', there is no absolute need for that child to know about Shakespeare? 'Absolutely correct,' answered Small, who was himself educated at Taunton School and Cambridge; princely pleas for a 'restoration of sanity' in the state school system leave him unruffled. 'We are responsible for seeing that every child has a chance to succeed. What is important is for books to be seen as a joy to turn to. The fact that it is Shakespeare is less important.'

Worse still for the panic-stricken traditionalists impatient for the proper teaching of the 'three Rs' and the reimposition of order, Small – and tens of thousands of teachers like him – believes that education has to do with 'enjoyment', 'enlisting enthusiasm' and 'thinking for yourself', not imposing discipline, whether of syllabus or behaviour. In the shadow of the Cowley car plant, Small looks forward to the day when children, continuing to leave school in droves at the first available opportunity, play an 'active negotiated part in their own education.'

No one at Cherwell comprehensive school with its 830 pupils aged from 13 to 18, 240 of them in the sixth form – seemed put out by the current gnashing of teeth about 'silly fashions' in education and the rending of raiment in high places about the future of 'our great literary heritage.' A 'mixed-ability' group of 13- to 14-year-olds, some lolling about, others mildly expectant, was being introduced by Peter Malin, head of English, to Chaucer.

'If you still have your coats on,' Malin said genially to the assembled jeans-and-trainers, 'could you take them off. Stand in the middle of the room', he continued in the clatter, 'and find a partner. Think of the most exciting thing you have done in the last two or three weeks, something really, really exciting.' (Minor outbreak of tittering, and no wonder.) 'Now tell your partner about it and explain it with more enthusiasm than you have ever done before.' (Cheerful bedlam; Chaucer wasn't done like this at Manchester Grammar.)

'Now I'm going to give each of you a piece of card,' Malin continued as the kids returned to their bare tables, 'with a series of words on it.' Each child had been given a different line from a passage in the Miller's Tale. 'I want you to speak the words to your partner as if they made real sense to you and with the same volume, energy and enthusiasm as when you were talking about your exciting experience.' (Renewed outbreak of chatter in mostly middle-class accents; this catchment area includes academic north Oxford.)

'Any ideas about what we've been reading?' asked Malin, 20 minutes into the lesson. 'Old English,' said Richard, chosen by Malin to answer. 'Would you like to put a date on it?' ('No', muttered a lad near me, sotto voce). 'Medieval period,' said mannerly Peter, also chosen. 'Anyone heard of any writer from that period?' 'Chaucer,' said Lebo from Soweto, unbidden.

When I left, they were reading their rhyming 22 lines from the Miller's Tale in correct sequence. 'I want you to discover,' Malin was saying enthusiastically – some still lolling, others bright eyed, one child fiddling with her hair – 'that you can understand what you didn't think you would understand when you first saw it.'

At Witney's Woodgreen comprehensive school, I saw 15-year-olds' GSCE essays not only on Romeo and Juliet ('The Montagues and Capulets could of [sic] pretended to be friends') but on Ben Elton's Stark and Alice Walker's The Color Purple. 'What if a kid wanted to do a project on the Beano?' I asked Jo Reid, head of English, who believes in 'guided personal choice' in matters of reading. 'It would depend what he or she wanted to do with it,' she answered. 'You could come at it in a very sophisticated fashion.'

Talk of 'culture' in the traditional sense will now get you nowhere at all. Indeed, for the traditionalist, 'treason has done its worst' to the notion that there is a body of received wisdom, and changed our schools beyond recognition.

'I don't want to produce people like me when I teach,' said Tim Small. Why not? 'Because it would be presumptuous,' he answered briskly. 'I celebrate diversity,' he added.

'Cultural heritage? It's a bit of a cliché,' said Malin. 'Handed down from on high,' said Small. 'If you have too much 'cultural heritage' you're not going to concentrate on today's issues,' said a bright sixth-former at Cherwell on her way to Cambridge. 'There's no point in studying something that was written ages ago just because it's old, if it's boring or stupid,' said a 15-year-old girl at Witney.

Yet it was also at Witney that I heard a lad struggle against the tide – 'rubbish' said another child while he was speaking – in an effort to articulate what it means to 'be English'. 'It's good to keep the old traditions,' he said to me, 'keep hold of the culture. Shakespeare is a good part of England.' 'Good, yes,' said another, 'but it shouldn't be forced on you.' 'It's the heritage,' he countered bravely, looking for words in an awkward, blushing moment, 'like fish and chips and football.'

Under the Southern Examining Group's regulations for GCSE English, Shakespeare is merely an option. Should it be so? I asked a group of 16- to 17-year-olds at Witney, setting out towards their A-levels. Isn't his writing at the heart of English culture?

'He was timeless,' said one. 'It is very important that you do read him at some stage. But I don't think he's the be-all and end-all. We study him for his genius, not because he is English culture.' 'Shakespeare is not just about national identity. He is a writer for the whole world,' declared another. These were fine young people, and what they said was both grand and touching. 'Shakespeare's alive and well in this school,' said Peter May, the headmaster.

With children such as these there is real hurt at the broad-brush implication of a generalised illiteracy stalking 'Shakespeare's land,' as Prince Charles put it. 'How can he say that about us?' said an irate 15-year-old at Witney, to general approval. 'When did he last spend a day in a school like this? Is he sending his children to a comprehensive?' Her own writing, which I saw later, contained words such as 'phrophercy' and 'domonate', but her reproach was proud and stinging.

Oh, what a battlefield this is, and how many the paradoxes of state eduction: of crassness and invention, of new dogma in the name of free-thinking, of dedicated amateurishness, true enlightenment and blind folly. 'I say to the staff,' declared Martin Roberts, head of Cherwell, 'don't let the great debate get you down.'

To the traditionalists, scrutinising the dire statistics of British educational failure, fair has been made foul, and foul fair, in an inversion of all values. To the young teachers in their staff rooms, products themselves of a now unchangeable order, the critic is seen as 'simply uninformed', about the 'real situation'. The kicking up of dust about the numbers of the 'culturally inept' is, for the most, distant sound and fury, signifying only prejudice against the comprehensive system.

As for the children themselves, they seem to know, unnervingly, that the prevailing wisdom of the 'experts' is not on the side either of 'tradition' or compulsion, but is predisposed to free-ranging innovation, however eccentric or unsuccessful. The older generation, I was told by a 15-year-old in Witney, 'can't relate. You were always barked at, and you did what you were told. We are not worried about saying anything. We can turn round and just say, "I don't agree".'

The ground they stand on, arm-in-arm with their teachers, may be – and in my view is – an educational quagmire. But it will not now be retaken.

*Yet it was also at Witney that I heard a lad struggle against the tide –
'rubbish' said another child while he was speaking – in an effort to
articulate what it means to 'be English.' (column 3)*

*These were fine, young people, and what they said was both grand and
touching. (column 3)*

*Her own writing, which I saw later, contained words such as 'phrophercy'
and 'domonate' . . . (column 3)*

*. . . of new dogma in the name of free-thinking, of dedicated
amateurishness, true enlightenment and blind folly. (column 3)*

*The ground they stand on, arm-in-arm with their teachers, may be – and
in my view is – an educational quagmire. But it will not now be retaken.
(column 3)*

(b) Are there any other extracts from the passage that shed light on
David Selbourne's views? And can you find any clues about his own
educational background that might have influenced him?

(c) Do you think David Selbourne visited the school with his mind
already made up? Does he attempt to be 'fair' and 'balanced'?

(d) No article could include all there is to say on a certain subject.
Nevertheless, are there any significant omissions? (For example,
should David Selbourne have visited the homes of children and
talked to parents?)

Assignments for writing

1 Select one topic that arouses strong feelings 'for' and 'against' among
the members of your class – it might be rules about the wearing of
school uniform or experimentation on animals to test newly
developed drugs. Each person in the class should write a short piece,
no more than a side of A4, that expresses his or her views. Finally,
the pieces of written work should be distributed among small groups
of the class who should:

• divide the pieces up into three categories: definite approval; strong
disapproval; a balance of two views;

• discuss where and how the writers reveal their own particular bias
and what use is made of evidence in the writing.

2 Imagine that you are a reporter visiting your school to write a feature about contemporary teaching styles and the response of students to what they are taught. The reporter has followed your class for a day at school. Write the article you think the reporter would produce in a feature for *The Sunday Times* (or any daily newspaper of your own choice). Invent your own headline.

WHERE IS IT?

There are lots of words that can be rearranged to form place names. For instance, did you know that *more* can become *Rome*, *ancestral* can be turned into *Lancaster* and that *Llanfairpwllgwyngyllgogery-chwyrndrobwllllantysiliogogogoch* becomes . . . well, we'll leave you to puzzle that one out. Here are some more manageable geographical anagrams for you to solve. We've given you some clues as to where the places are.

Hasten (European capital)   At Sex (US state)

Roved (Kent port)   Planes (Italian city)

Lost rib (English city)   No gore (US state)

Serial (Middle-Eastern country)   Throwing (English coast town)

No seal's leg (US city)   Pairs (European capital)

Mail (South American capital)   Nerviness (Scottish city)

Salvages (US city)   Rock (Irish city)

Chapter Fifteen

GENRE

BUNGLING COPS IN 4am SWOOP ON FAMILY

You won't have had any difficulty in recognising that this is a newspaper headline. In fact, it's a headline from *The Sun*. Although you wouldn't have been entirely certain that it came from *The Sun* rather than, say the *Daily Star*, you'd have been unlikely to identify it as coming from *The Times* or the *Guardian*.

But just *how* did you recognise it as a tabloid headline? We haven't enclosed the whole of *The Sun* in this book, so you couldn't have recognised it from its context. There must be something about both the subject matter and the language that says to you 'I'm a tabloid newspaper headline!' What? Here are a few of the reasons that might have helped:

- Slang term for *police* used.
- Only eight words altogether.
- No verbs.
- All words in capital letters.
- Large type.
- No *a* or *the* used. Just *Family*.
- Dramatic words used like *swoop* and *bungling*.

In fact, most people are skilled readers and usually find it easy to identify very different types of writing, just as you did with the headline. What is more difficult is to say *how* they knew what the writing was. It's not enough to say, 'Well, I just knew. It's obvious, isn't it?'

On the next few pages, you will find extracts from various types of writing. You may recognise some of the types as easily as you did the headline. Some may not be quite so simple. For each extract, see if you can identify the type of writing and say what were the features that helped you make the identification. To help you when you are discussing these features, here are some questions that you can ask. In fact, you can use them about *any* text, not just the ones here.

1 What is the text about? (People? Individual or groups? Things? Ideas?)

2 What is the writer's purpose? (Persuade? Inform? Instruct? Entertain? A mixture of these?)

3 Who is the text written for? (You? Someone else? One person? A group? Experts? Old people? Young people?)

4 What does the text look like? (Layout? Typefaces used?)

5 How is the text organised? (Bullet points? Paragraphs? Headings/sub-headings? How do the sections of the text link?)

6 What types of words are used? (Formal? Informal? Everyday ones? Taken from specialised subject area?)

7 Are there any noticeable grammatical features?

8 Does it remind you of similar texts? (In what way?)

THEY BULLY ME

I'm 13 and get bullied all the time. I know I'm a little weird, but I have feelings too. People in my class pick on me for every little thing. I am very thin, so they call me twig; I wear a brace, so they call me metal mouth. I know they are only doing it for a laugh, and I try to laugh it off, but it makes me feel really bad. Why is this happening? I just want to be the same as the others.

Anon, Lancs

Bullies always need a scapegoat. This is usually a person who has been singled out and is blamed for anything and everything. No one deserves to be called horrible names and have their life made a misery. You are in no way to blame for any of this, which is why you must tell someone what's going on. Speaking to a teacher or your parents is the only way to put an end to this bullying. You need someone in authority to make a stand. It can – and must – be stopped.

Priority Booking Number: 374415

September 1995

Dear Mr Eustice

ANTARCTICA - THE ULTIMATE CHRISTMAS HOLIDAY!

Imagine you are on board the luxurious cruise-ship Marco Polo .....
..... you are under a blue sky with the sun reflected on a sparkling sea. As you sail past icebergs and glaciers in Antarctica's Lemaire Channel, you pinch yourself to make sure you are not dreaming.....
..... is it really Christmas Eve? ... was I really walking beside penguins yesterday? ...am I really surrounded by all this beauty .... glaciers, icebergs, and the stunning art-deco design that distinguishes the Marco Polo as one of the magnificent ships of the world.

Imagine the thrill of going ashore by Zodiac during the day to visit penguin colonies.... the excitement of seeing whales.... an aperitif in the Polo Lounge piano bar in the late afternoon.... then a superb dinner in the Seven Seas Restaurant. Could this all really be possible?

The answer is 'yes!' Because in December 1995 the Marco Polo is going to take passengers on the Christmas holiday of a lifetime. After 3 nights' stay in a first-class hotel in vibrant Buenos Aires, you could embark the Marco Polo to cruise to the Falkland Islands and across the Drake Passage to the Peninsula of the White Continent itself - Antarctica.

GOODFOOD & SAFEWAY MAGAZINE

Balti-Style Turkey Curry

all you need from Safeway is...

15ml/1 tbsp vegetable oil
4 Safeway turkey breast steaks, cut into 2cm/¾ in pieces
1 yellow and 1 red pepper, seeded and cut into 2cm/¾ in pieces
2 small carrots, diagonally sliced
100g/4oz fine green beans, halved
75g/3oz frozen peas
45ml/3 tbsp mild curry paste
410g can Carnation Evaporated Milk
50g/2oz Blue Dragon Coconut Powder
fresh coriander sprigs, to garnish
Batchelors Delicately Flavoured Pilau rice, to serve

1 Heat the oil in a large frying pan or wok and stir fry the turkey for 3 minutes. Add the peppers, carrots and green beans and stir fry for a further 2 minutes.

2 Stir in the peas, curry paste and evaporated milk. Bring to a gentle simmer and cook for 2 minutes, stirring occasionally.

3 Sprinkle over the coconut powder and stir to dissolve. Continue to simmer gently for 3 minutes until the vegetables and turkey are tender, stirring often. Garnish with coriander and serve with pilau rice.

Cook's tip

Serve this curry with freshly boiled pilau rice or warmed naan bread.

Use special Balti stir fry curry paste for this recipe if you like, or try medium or hot curry paste instead.
You can also use Carnation Lite Evaporated Milk for a lower fat alternative.

Wine Suggestion

Safeway Sparkling Cava, 75cl. Available at most Safeway stores.

 Family Meal

Serves : 4
Preparation time : 10-15 mins

If you would like any other recipe cards in this collection
Items subject to availability

Re-transmitting clock data

Clock data is retained in the remote control after it is transmitted to the VCR. If the VCR's clock data cancelled (because of a power failure etc.), or if the data is wrong, the clock data in the remote control can be re-transmitted to the VCR.

1 Press the CLOCK button.
The year will appear on the LC display.

2 Point the remote control's transmitter at the VCR's remote sensor window and press the TRANSMIT button to transmit the clock data.
Transmit indicator will light on the LC display to indicate that the data has been transmited.

3 Press the CLOCK button to return the remote control to its normal mode.

Gypsy Colt

10.25am-11.40am BBC2
10.25-11.40 (75 mins)

Is there a 13-year-old horse-mad daughter in the house? If so, get those Kleenex at the ready for this endearing if rather treacly tale. A young horse owner is reduced to despair by her parents' decision to sell her much-loved pet to a highfalutin racing stables, but love will out, even when it's on four sturdy legs. This is a highly professional film which presses all the right buttons, but is no less effective for that.
(US 1954)
★★★.........................5934175

House of Strangers

2.05pm-4.00pm C4
14.05-16.00 (115 mins)

This drama features Edward G Robinson as a man who achieves the American Dream by becoming a successful banker but is then arrested for malpractice. Three of his sons take over and prevent him from resuming his responsibilities when he's released. Richard Conte's affair with Susan Hayward is a dramatic dead end and you feel the picture would have been better as a gangster thriller about the Mafia. Despite these flaws, Robinson's performance and the subversive theme make it well worth watching. *(US 1949) b/w ◆*
★★★.........................779446

Blue Fire Lady

2.20pm-3.55pm BBC2
14.20-15.55 (95 mins)

Made in those forgettable seventies when Australia was just emerging from years of this type of anthropomorphic nonsense, this is the story of a girl and her love for a racehorse who seems to know her every whim and mood, as they do. This is a film with so much soft focus you'll think your bi-focals have misted up. The young will love it but cynical adults should beware. *(Aus 1977)*
★★.............................422473

Brubaker

10.00pm-12.25am C4
22.00-00.25 (145 mins)

Robert Redford in reformist mode, as the new warden trying to oust brutality and corruption from a state prison farm. Director Stuart Rosenberg pile-drives on the pile-driving agony with strokes of solid action, while the acting – Jane Alexander and Yaphet Kotto, especially – is formidable enough to take on all that social responsibility. A touch downbeat, as when it goes underground to expose past horrors, it sounds a shrill warning for all. Ponderous and sanctimonious at times, but still an ominous message for all who care about what we do with our misfits. A universal cause for concern. Contains violence and swearing. *(US 1980, 15*)*
★★★★.....................40845311

A Warm Welcome to Knutsford

Knutsford, an historic town, rich in heritage, brimming with variety and friendly surprises - 'ginnels, cobbles and courtyards' to explore from 'Top Street' to 'Bottom Street', boutiques to antiques, purveyors of wines, cheese and herbs, to galleries of art, interior design and houses for 'the little people'.

Relax and enjoy quality restaurants, coffee houses and inns - a choice to satisfy all.

Knutsford

Be a successful writer
Make money writing - even while you are learning

HOW DOES IT WORK?

Top professional writers give you *individual* tuition as you work through the School's comprehensive home-study course. You are given assignments to complete *at your own pace* and these are edited and commented on by your own tutor, who works with you on a *one-to-one* basis.

You get personal tips that have taken years to evolve and which are passed on with astonishing results.

There's no real pleasure in writing unless you can get published. Seeing your own words in print is unforgettably satisfying. And if you're actually paid, too, you *know* that other people recognise the quality of your writing.

Since 1949, The Writing School has been teaching people how to write articles, short stories, novels, romances, radio and TV scripts. Equally important, we've been teaching students how to *sell* what they write.

"AM I REALLY QUALIFIED?"

If you want to write and are reasonably literate, yes. In fact, if you've read this far, there's no doubt of your capability to take the course.

If you have a serious ambition to write you can gain invaluable help from the School. And, what's more, you'll find the whole process enjoyable, too!

"The reason for this success is my tutor, who has constructively criticised my work and given me invaluable help and assistance."
M.L.Lowestoft

"I must say a few words in praise of my tutor. He has been excellent, first class in his guidance and his gentle remarks have contained an immense amount of professional knowledge which is sometimes difficult to understand from reading books."
J.S.Cardiff

"The Writing School has given me a chance to break the ice into a career in writing. Whether the published piece of work is small or major, the most important thing at the end of the day is to see your name in print."
V.O'M.County Mayo, Eire

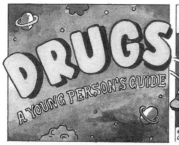

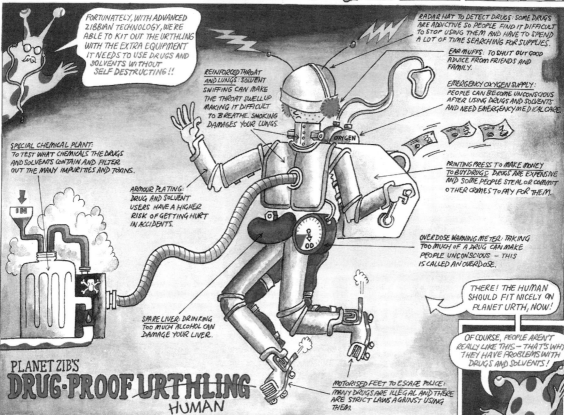

WHAT IS GENRE?

One of the reasons that you probably found it easy to identify both the headline from *The Sun* and some of the texts you have just been discussing is that you are familiar with these types of writing. Another word for *type* or *sort* is **genre**. There are lots of genres. Novels, for example, can be divided into:

- detective stories
- thrillers
- historical novels
- science-fiction
- Mills and Boon romances
- spy stories

and so on. Each one of these is a genre: a type of writing (or speech) that we can identify by its distinctive subject matter and the way it's written. Of course, genres aren't restricted to fiction. Look at these: textbooks, sermons, weather forecasts, songs, diaries, questionnaires, drama scripts, telephone conversations, jokes . . . you could go on and add lots of examples to this list. All are genres.

Another way of considering genres is to think of them as a family relationship. Most members of a family share certain characteristics: hair colour, complexion, height are just some of the ways in which people can be recognised as belonging to the same family, but this doesn't mean that the family members are identical. It's just like that with genres. For instance, magazine problem pages have many of the same characteristics, but you wouldn't mistake a problem page from *More* for one from *Woman's Weekly*. Families can have family trees: so can genres. Look at this (incomplete) 'family tree' we drew up for music:

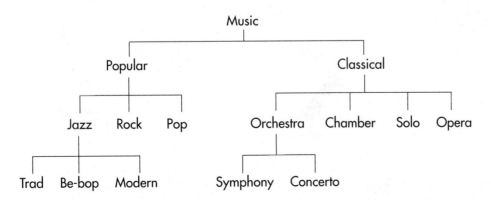

You might not agree with the way we have divided music up and could come up with a better 'family tree' than this, but the point is that though Trad Jazz and Chamber are types of music and thus belong to the same extended family, they have distinctly different sounds from each other and thus can be called different genres.

> Draw up 'genre-trees' of your own. You can decide on your own subjects, expand on the music tree or choose a subject from this list:
>
> newspapers; fiction; jokes; letters; magazines; persuasive writing; poetry, talk.

GENRE BENDING

You can come up with some rather odd and amusing effects by playing around with genres. We've suggested that a genre is recognised by both its style and its subject matter, but if you mix the style of one genre with the subject matter of another, there's plenty of potential for humour. A weather forecast in rap, for example. Or what about a geography exam paper in the style of a travel brochure? You'll be able to think of lots more examples of your own.

To show you what can be done by mixing genres, we've given you three amusing (we hope) illustrations. They're all based on the nursery rhyme *Jack and Jill*, but you'll see that it's not the short version with which you are familiar, but a nineteenth-century one with several additional verses.

THE ADVENTURES OF JACK AND JILL
AND OLD DAME GILL

Jack and Jill
Went up the hill,
To fetch a pail of water;
Jack fell down,
And broke his crown,
And Jill came tumbling after.

Then up Jack got,
And home did trot,
As fast as he could caper;
Dame Gill did the job,
To plaster his nob
With vinegar and brown paper.

Then Jill came in,
And she did grin
To see Jack's paper plaster;
Her mother, vexed,
Did whip her next,
For laughing at Jack's disaster.

This made Jill pout,
And she ran out,
And Jack did quickly follow;
They rode dog Ball
Till Jill did fall,
Which made Jack laugh and halloo.

Then Dame came out
To enquire about,
Jill said Jack made her tumble;
Says Jack, I'll tell
You how she fell,
Then judge if she need grumble.

Dame Gill did grin
As she went in,
And Jill was plagued by Jack;
Will Goat came by,
And made Jack cry,
And knocked him on his back.

Though Jack wasn't hurt,
He was all over dirt;
I wish you had but seen him,
And how Jill did jump
Towards the pump,
And pumped on him to clean him.

Which done, all three
Went in to tea,
And put the place all right;
Which done, they sup,
Then take a cup,
And wish you a good night.

JACK'S PAIL AFTER NHS CUTBACKS

By MICHAEL SHARPE

Further details on p.

1   Local TV news report

Following an accident at Watery Hill, Wilmslow, Jill Smythe-Johnstone, 10, of The Aspens, Nursery Close, was immediately admitted for observation as a private patient in the neurological ward.

However, when Jack Stringer, 10, of The Backs, Brick Row, arrived at the casualty department two hours later, after a distressing bus journey during which his mother had to staunch the flow of blood from his head wound, he found it closed as a result of National Health Service cuts, and although clearly badly concussed, was forced to return home without treatment.

The hospital's spokesman denied the allegations, insisting that Mrs Stringer had been informed that the casualty department at St Mary's Hospital, only an eight mile bus journey away, was open for emergencies. Our reporter spoke with Mr Smythe-Johnstone.

(CUT to outside broadcast team. Reporter standing with Mr Smythe-Johnstone at hospital gates, BUPA sign clearly visible.)

Mr S-J: *My daughter was quite badly shaken, but, having spent the night under observation in a private room, she seems to have recovered.*

(CUT to living room of Stringer home where second reporter is interviewing Mrs Ada Stringer.)

Mrs Stringer: *When they cut off the water, I didn't think it would come to this. Our Jack's been waiting to go in to have his knee done for over a year. I'd have gone private if I'd had the money, but with Jack's dad on the sick, there's no chance. And now he's gone and done his head as well.*

Reporter: *But . . . vinegar and brown paper, Mrs Stringer?*

Mrs Stringer: *It was all we had in. The men swore by it.*

(CUT to studio.)

Newsreader: *The Shadow Minister for Health, Harriet Harman, commented 'The government is once again papering over the cracks in the National Health Service.'*

2 American 'hard-boiled' detective novel

THE BIG KISS-OFF OF JACK AND JILL

It was a Thursday morning and I had lots to do, like stare out of my window. I heard my outer office door open, and turned to see a blonde girl, maybe twenty-five years old.

'You can come right in,' I called.
She straightened her skirt and walked in very quickly. She was tall and composed, with a perfect nose, absolutely perfect.
'You're Levine, PI?'
'I am if you want me.'
'My man Jack needs your help.'
I couldn't have cared less. I cared more when she slowly crossed her legs.
'I hardly know where to begin, Mr Levine.'
'Begin at the dirty part. It's been a slow week.'
'Jack and I are co-starring in The Grand Old Duke of York*: we were shooting the hill scene. You know he's a big matinee star, but he's been drinking more lately. He's got something on his mind.'*

'Blackmail?' I interposed. Her open, blue jacket revealed a tight sweater that was being stretched to its limits.

'That's for you to find out. He's playing the king and he was real tipsy last night. When it got to the bit when we had to fetch a pail of water, he fell down and broke his crown. And I just fell right down there with him.'

The thought of those long, lithe limbs intertwined with Jack's drove me crazy.

'Then up Jack got. And I rushed him to the condo in a cab. Fortunately, we'd got in a stock of vinegar and brown paper. And I got on with the job of plastering his nob.'

'You did what?

3 Children's school science textbook

JACK AND JILL

QUESTIONS

1 Gravity is the force which pulls everything down towards the earth. Explain why Jack falls down. Could Jack every fall up? If not, why not?

2 Draw a simple diagram showing where Jack's head is in relation to the ground.

3 Why is Jack likely to fall while he is carrying a bucket of water downhill?

4 Vinegar is mild acid. Do you think it is likely to help heal Jack's head? Why do you think Dame Gill used it to help him? How much vinegar do you think would be needed to soak the brown paper? You could experiment for yourself.

5 Explain why the well is more likely to be at the top of the hill than in the valley.

6 What reasons can you think of to explain why Jill fell down after Jack?

7 Jack makes his way home at a 'trot' and 'caper'. Which is likely to get him home faster and why?

8 Why do you think that Jack and Jill are children? Do you think that adults would behave in the same way?

9 What remedies would we use today to cure Jack's head?

10 Explain how you get water in your house.

Jack and Jill extracts – School of Education, Leeds University

Try writing your own genre-bending versions of *Jack and Jill*. Here are a few suggestions to spark off your own ideas.

- CD booklet for *Jack and Jill*, new rock musical;
- TV Times article about a new children's serial, *Jack and Jill*;
- Jill's diary entries;
- script of TV advert for *Gripperwell*, a new brand of children's non-slip shoes;
- blurb for *Head Over Heels*, a romantic blockbuster novel based on *Jack and Jill*;
- letter from and reply to Jill in *Confidential*, the problem page of *Just 17*;
- article in *The Sun*;
- advertisement for a new brand of tea, *The Cup That Cheers*;
- magazine profile of star who plays Jack/Jill in new Hollywood film about the trials of young love;
- article in serious newspaper about revolutionary new medical treatment – vinegar and brown paper.

You need not confine yourself to writing on *Jack and Jill*. Lots of other nursery rhymes can be rewritten. What about *Hey Diddle, Diddle, the Cat and the Fiddle, Four and Twenty Blackbirds* or *Little Miss Muffet*? Or fairy tales and children's stories? *The Three Billy Goats Gruff? Cinderella? Little Red Riding Hood? Goldilocks and the Three Bears?* Then there are poems that appeal to children: *The Owl and the Pussycat, Jabberwocky, The Pied Piper of Hamelin*. The list is almost endless.

HOW MANY?

How many words can you make from each of these nine-letter words? You can only use each letter once, the words must be of three letters or more and proper nouns or foreign words are not allowed. Apart from that, anything goes – as long as the word is in a dictionary!

Aborigine (real brainboxes can find seventy-four words!)

Inaudible	Ornaments	Chocolate
Fictional	Primitive	Triumphal
Cigarette	Billiards	